Popular Mechanics

do-it-yourself encyclopedia

The complete, illustrated home reference guide from the world's most authoritative source for today's how-to-do-it information.

Volume 7

DARKROOM PROJECTS
to
DRAWING

HEARST DIRECT BOOKS

NEW YORK

Acknowledgements

The Popular Mechanics Encyclopedia is published with the consent and cooperation of POPULAR MECHANICS Magazine.

For POPULAR MECHANICS Magazine:

Editor-in-Chief: *Joe Oldham*
Managing Editor: *Bill Hartford*
Special Features Editor: *Sheldon M. Gallager*
Automotive Editor: *Wade A. Hoyt, SAE*
Home and Shop Editor: *Steve Willson*
Electronics Editor: *Stephen A. Booth*
Boating, Outdoors and Travel Editor: *Timothy H. Cole*
Science Editor: *Dennis Eskow*

Popular Mechanics Encyclopedia

Project Director: *Boyd Griffin*
Manufacturing: *Ron Schoenfeld*
Assistant Editors: *Cynthia W. Lockhart, Peter McCann, Rosanna Petruccio*
Production Coordinator: *Peter McCann*

The staff of Popular Mechanics Encyclopedia is grateful to the following individuals and organizations:

Editor: *C. Edward Cavert*
Editor Emeritus: *Clifford B. Hicks*
Production: *Layla Productions*
Production Director: *Lori Stein*
Book Design: *The Bentwood Studio*
Art Director: *Jos. Trautwein*
Design Consultant: *Suzanne Bennett & Associates*
Illustrations: *AP Graphics, Evelyne Johnson Associates, Popular Mechanics Magazine, Vantage Art.*

Contributing Writers: James L. Abbott, *Darkroom in a suitcase,* page 776; Clarence E. Banister, *Lightbox you can build inexpensively,* page 886; Walter E. Burton, *Fun with a doodling engraver,* page 892; Rosario Capotosto, *Campaign desk,* page 824; *Rolltop desk for nostalgia buffs,* page 830; *Dining room set,* page 839; *Mini-maxi gateleg table,* page 852; C. Wayne Close, *Stamp and pencil set,* page 807; Frank H. Day, *Perpetual desk calendar,* page 805; Louis J. Dilullo, *Colonial trestle desk,* page 821; Everett Johnson, *Trestle table,* page 845; Raymond D. Johnson, *Darkroom for your bathroom that rolls away,* page 772; Elbert Lawton, *Darkroom in borrowed space,* page 773; Joshua Mark, *Deck on two levels for entertaining,* page 799; Bob Tom, *Scribe large circles the easy way,* page 891; Joseph Truini, *Deck for anywhere,* page 788; Harry Wicks, *Decks you can build,* page 779; *Deck on two levels for entertaining,* page 799; *Victorian sideboard,* page 856; *Dollhouse is a toy box too,* page 864; *Sliding glass doors let the outdoors in,* page 877.

Photographic Credits: California Redwood Association, pages 779, 785 and 792 (Deck); Georgia-Pacific Corporation, page 785 (top).

ISBN 0-87851-160-1

Library of Congress 85-81760

10 9 8 7 6 5 4 3 2 1
PRINTED IN THE UNITED STATES OF AMERICA

Although every effort has been made to ensure the accuracy and completeness of the information in this book, Hearst Direct Books makes no guarantees, stated or implied, nor will they be liable in the event of misinterpretation or human error made by the reader, or for any typographical errors that may appear. WORK SAFELY WITH HAND TOOLS. WEAR SAFETY GOGGLES. READ MANUFACTURER'S INSTRUCTIONS AND WARNINGS FOR ALL PRODUCTS.

Contents

Darkroom for your bathroom that rolls away

■ THIS QUICK-CHANGE SETUP turns a 5x8 bathroom into a handy darkroom in less than five minutes. If someone wants a fast shower, you can have the whole works knocked down and stored away in the same short time.

Heart of the system is a roll-around unit that houses enlarger, print dryer, processing trays, paper, paper cutter and chemicals—all in a compact, counter-height cabinet only 20 in. wide by 24 in. deep. Ball glides on the bottom make it easy to move. Rolled into the bathroom, it becomes a stand for the enlarger, and a single-legged table hooks onto the side for added work space. The cabinet can be stored in a closet or parked in the kitchen.

Completing the setup is a drop-down counter hinged to the wall above the tub. This swings up and rests on a shower-curtain rod slipped into holders on the side walls. When not in use, the rod stores in a duplicate set of holders mounted near the back wall out of the way. The counter is purposely made slightly shallower than the tub so spills run off into the tub instead of on the floor.

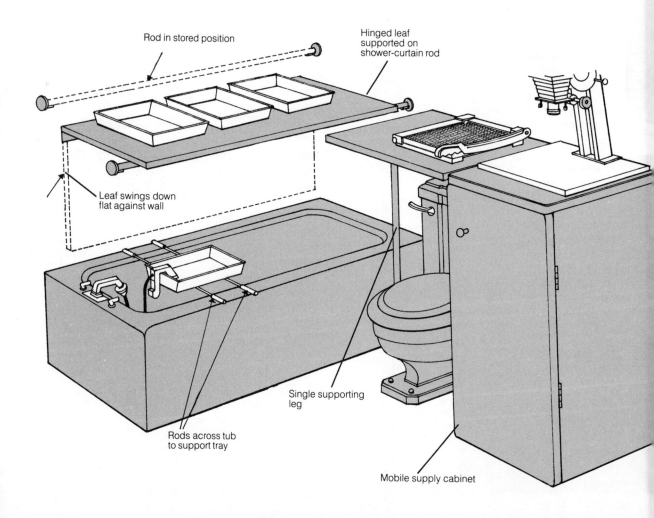

Rod in stored position

Hinged leaf supported on shower-curtain rod

Leaf swings down flat against wall

Single supporting leg

Rods across tub to support tray

Mobile supply cabinet

Darkroom in borrowed space

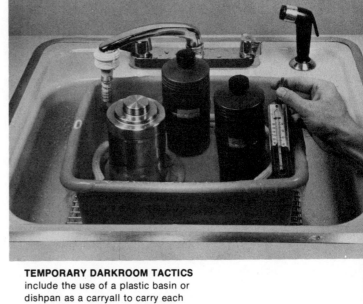

TEMPORARY DARKROOM TACTICS include the use of a plastic basin or dishpan as a carryall to carry each night's equipment to your workroom. It can also be used as a temperature-control bath (as shown above) and finally as a washer.

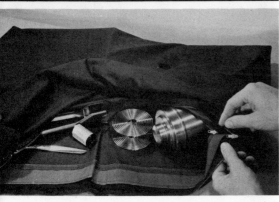

■ IN MOST HOMES, finding space for a permanent darkroom is very difficult. When faced with this situation, many photographers find it easier to borrow space somewhere around the house for a few hours. One of the problems they encounter is that they are losing half their time setting up and taking down all the equipment which is necessary for developing and printing. If this is a problem you face, portable darkroom equipment and a work plan are what you need. The first rule is to keep everything as simple as possible. Buy and use only the essentials—"time-saving" luxuries will seem a lot less luxurious if the time saved is then spent in moving them from place to place. Some photographers fear that using just the essentials

THE PHOTO shows how a changing bag can be used for loading film-developing tanks of many different sizes.

will mean they can't do as good a job as someone with a permanent setup. This isn't true! However, it does mean that you can't count on quite as many prints per evening without cutting quality.

The second rule is to compartmentalize your work. This will involve careful planning as it simply isn't practical to drag out and set up *everything* each time you have a free hour or two to work.

It's better to break your darkroom work down into separate stages. Each of these stages can then be served by its own equipment and supplies. You can divide your darkroom work into four such stages: chemical mixing; film processing; printing and print processing; and print drying, spotting and mounting. Limit yourself to one stage per work session (with the possible exception of the mixing stage). By using a method such as this you will find you accomplish a lot more than if you try to do everything at once.

Mixing the chemicals

Chemical preparation takes little space and can be done in full room light. You can usually mix your chemicals the night you plan to use them, especially if you go to pre-mixed or liquid chemicals. Many powdered chemicals are supposed to be mixed at temperatures much higher than the standard 68°F. processing temperature. Mix them before dinner, and they'll be down to room temperature by the time you're ready for work.

You have the choice of the one-shot developers that are discarded after use or the kind you replenish. Some people prefer the one-shot developers as they're fresh each time—important when you do only occasional darkroom work.

Your equipment for this stage should include a quart graduate for measuring and mixing, a two-ounce graduate for adding replenisher (if you use it), a long-stem bar mixing spoon or mixing paddle, a funnel, a thermometer and plastic bottles. Some chemicals, which age more slowly (such as fixer and hypo eliminator), can be mixed more economically and conveniently in gallon quantities. This is especially true of fixer, which goes fast. If you do mix a gallon, divide it into quart bottles—the chemicals in the unopened bottles will last even longer, and you'll have less weight to lug around. If you can, always use separate graduates and paddles for mixing developer and fixer; otherwise, wash extra carefully between chemicals to keep one from contaminating the other.

Probably the best place in the house to do your mixing is the kitchen sink. And to carry your chemicals and equipment from storage to the sink and back, use a plastic dishpan—it will come in handy again in the next stage.

Now you are ready to do the actual developing. Developing film requires just a little additional equipment: a daylight-type developing tank, film reels, a changing bag, scissors, a length of hose (optional) from a bathroom hair-sprayer attachment, and (if you use 35-mm film) either a cassette opener or bottle-cap opener. The basic chemicals you'll need are film developer, stop bath (optional) and fixer. To speed up your processing, you can use rapid fixer instead of regular "hypo" type and a hypo neutralizer between fixing and washing to reduce washing time. Dip your film in wetting agent to speed up drying a bit and reduce the formation of water spots on the film.

Use a changing bag as a "dark-room." You will find that it is just big enough to hold the film, tank and reels. You can load the tank at your convenience.

Plastic dishpan is useful

When developing, your plastic dishpan can serve double duty as a carry-all to bring your paraphernalia to the kitchen sink and as a water jacket. Filled with water at 68°F., it will bring all the chemicals and the tank to the correct temperature and hold them there for a period of time.

The best way to wash the film is to use a faucet's attached hose to direct a strong jet of water (still at 68°) through the center of the reels down to the bottom of the tank, where it will flush any impurities away. Some tanks come with hose assemblies, but with a little tinkering the hair-spray hose mentioned earlier seems to work well with many different kinds of tanks.

Printing takes a bit more equipment. You will need a developer and stop-bath tray at least as big as the largest prints you'll make as well as a larger tray for the fixing bath. You will also need tongs to agitate prints and carry them from one tray to another, and finally another deep plastic basin drilled with holes to serve as a washer.

Of course, you'll also need an enlarger and lenses for it. Unless you're sure you'll be shooting just 35-mm or 126 Instamatic photos for the rest of your life, it pays to buy the 35-mm-to-120 size—it won't be much more expensive. Look for one that can be disassembled easily for compact storage, but that is still of quality construction. The quality of your enlarger will directly affect the quality of your prints. If you want to get good sharp prints, buy a well-built enlarger. This is no place to save money.

You'll need enlarging lenses, too. You should get a 2-inch lens for 35-mm, or a 3-inch lens for 120 negatives. If you're trying to print both sizes but can only afford one lens at first, use a 3-inch lens, and attach a close-up lens to its front when you need bigger enlargements.

In enlarging easels, your best bet is the kind with calibrated, adjustable masking bands that let you use different paper sizes or crop your borders to precisely match the shape of your image. Most photographers agree that not all photos look best in precise 8x10 proportions. Look for an easel whose masking bands are supported on all four sides, not flopping in the air when you raise them to insert the paper. You should begin with an 8x10-size easel. Even after making bigger enlargements, you'll probably find that this size is easier to use when working with smaller prints.

Do without some "nonessentials"

The only essential accessory left is a safelight. If you were setting up a permanent darkroom you would surely want to include such things as enlarging timers, paper safes and focusing magnifiers. But with your portable darkroom, you can do without them at first. Count seconds aloud (say "one-hippopotamus, two-hippopotamus . . ." to space the seconds properly) or watch the kitchen clock's sweep second hand. You can remove the paper sheets one at a time from the box, placing your body as a shield between the open box and the safelight. The focus can be checked with a conventional magnifier.

Once you have all your printing equipment ready, you are faced with the question of where and how you should set it up. For the "where" you have several choices: A basement location near the utility sink will minimize disruption of your family's life, provided the location is comfortable and free of dust. The kitchen is the next best bet because of its deep sink and its counter-top space—but you'll have to wait till the dishes are washed, and teach everyone to knock before coming in. The bathroom is least preferable, since its sink is too small, its tub too low, and you'll frequently have to stop to admit other family members.

A sink isn't really needed till the final wash, though, so you can set up in a dry room—pick one with lots of space, few windows and low family traffic—just by adding another dishpan full

of water to hold the prints till you can take a batch of them outside for washing.

Whatever room you pick, make sure it has a sturdy table or counter that won't shake under your enlarger. Keep your "dry" operations (enlarging and paper storage) separate from wet ones (developing, stop bath and fixing), either on opposite sides of the room or with a partition between them.

All that's left is darkness—and you need that only for enlarging. For daylight processing, cover the windows with large, black plastic trash bags from the supermarket, the red-brown type will do for use at night.

It is very important that the entire room be light-tight. If the room has a door, make it light-tight with weatherstripping. If not, cover the open doorway with more plastic, overlapping and taping the bags together. Carefully look to make sure there is no other light leaking into the room. At this point, ventilation can be a problem. A kitchen fan will handle the problem for you.

Print drying can be left to the day after your printing session. It won't hurt the prints to soak, though the water should be changed a few times. Squeeze an electric print-dryer into your budget if at all possible—it's the only way to make sure that the prints you've spent hours making will look as good when dry as they did wet. For matte prints, you'll get a far more smoothly finished, wrinkle-free surface than you could with a blotter; and with ferrotype tins, you'll get good glossy prints much faster than you would with plain air drying. The best size for your dryer of ferrotype tins is 16x20 inches. It's big enough to handle big prints and will let you dry four 8x10s at once.

The finishing touches

For finishing touches, take the extra steps of spotting and mounting your prints. With just three bottles of spotting tone (in different densities) and a fine brush, you can render many dust spots and other imperfections invisible. For print-mounting, your best bet is to use one of the special adhesives sold in photo stores. Electric dry-mounting presses are bulky and expensive, and though a few hobbyists dry-mount successfully with a clothes iron, there's risk of damage to the print.

Useful mounting tools include a wallboard knife, a steel straightedge for trimming, and a board with a weight on top to press the paper down for a blemish-free surface.

Darkroom in a suitcase

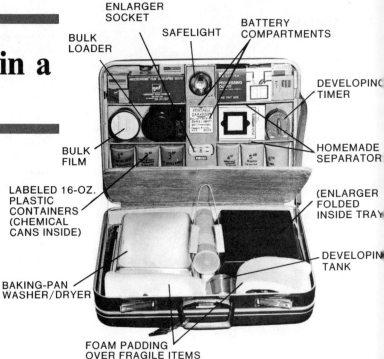

ENLARGER SOCKET

BULK LOADER

SAFELIGHT

BATTERY COMPARTMENTS

DEVELOPING TIMER

BULK FILM

HOMEMADE SEPARATOR

LABELED 16-OZ. PLASTIC CONTAINERS (CHEMICAL CANS INSIDE)

(ENLARGER FOLDED INSIDE TRAY)

DEVELOPING TANK

BAKING-PAN WASHER/DRYER

FOAM PADDING OVER FRAGILE ITEMS

IN THE SUITCASE is a complete darkroom outfit, cleverly tucked away in homebuilt compartments, or one item inside another item.

■ EVER COME BACK from vacation only to find you or your camera hadn't been shooting properly, or that the local lab had finished *off* your pictures instead of finishing them?

You can prevent that from ever happening to you again. You can take your darkroom with you—in one ordinary "two-suiter" suitcase measuring only 7 by 17 by 24 in. and weighing less than 35 lbs. Within minutes you can set it up (even where no electricity is available) and start developing your day's color slide, or developing and printing black and white. If you've missed anything important, you'll know in plenty of time to reshoot the next day.

The case shown here is adapted specifically to the equipment illustrated. You'll have to adjust its dimensions to your own.

The first principle is packing the minimum equipment. Use the smallest enlarger you can find. Many small 35-mm enlargers on the market today disassemble quickly for packing. For U.S. travel, that and good quality are about the only requirements. For foreign travel, you might try to find an imported enlarger that can adapt to Europe's higher voltages (about 240 volts). You can get around that by replacing your enlarger lamp and socket with a 6-volt flash-lantern bulb for battery operation here, abroad or outdoors. But be careful when you mount the new bulb to be

UNBELIEVABLE AMOUNTS of darkroom gear can fit in case; compact, take-apart enlarger is the key item.

sure its center is exactly where the old bulb's center was; otherwise your prints won't be evenly exposed.

The safelight is built into the case lid. It is a 12-volt truck running light with an orange lens. Two 6-volt lantern batteries in compartments in the lid power both the enlarger and the safelight. Running the enlarger's 6-volt bulb on 12 volts increases its brightness; it also shortens the bulb's life—carry extras—but not too much, since the enlarger usually runs for only seconds at a time.

For chemical mixing and storage, use 16-oz. plastic tumblers with lids. They're unbreakable, and they easily hold small chemical cans, or foam-wrapped breakables such as small bottles and thermometers.

For a print washer, use a 9 by 12-in. backing pan with a string of 1/8-in. drain holes drilled half an inch below each edge; water comes from a faucet hose into a 3/8-in. pipe with a capped end and 1/16-in. holes drilled in a row along it. For a dryer, invert this same pan over a low heat source (candle, catalytic heater or stove) and lay a ferrotype plate atop it; the drain holes now serve as

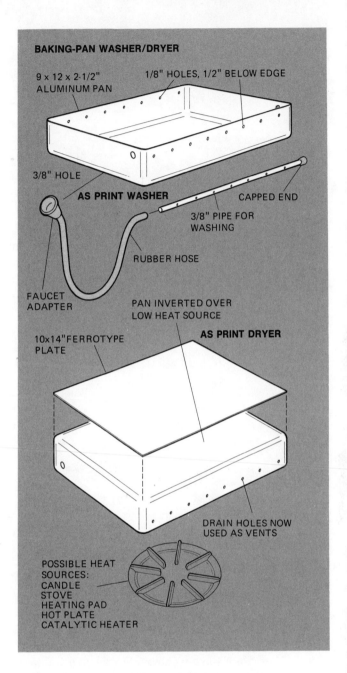

BAKING-PAN WASHER/DRYER

9 x 12 x 2-1/2" ALUMINUM PAN

1/8" HOLES, 1/2" BELOW EDGE

3/8" HOLE

AS PRINT WASHER

CAPPED END

3/8" PIPE FOR WASHING

RUBBER HOSE

FAUCET ADAPTER

PAN INVERTED OVER LOW HEAT SOURCE

10x14" FERROTYPE PLATE

AS PRINT DRYER

DRAIN HOLES NOW USED AS VENTS

POSSIBLE HEAT SOURCES: CANDLE STOVE HEATING PAD HOT PLATE CATALYTIC HEATER

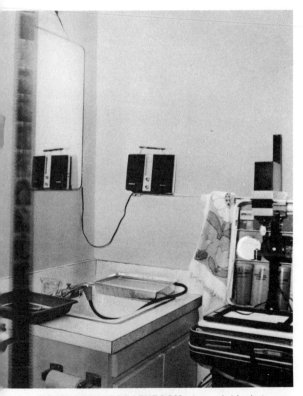

BATHROOM INTO DARKROOM takes only blankets over the windows, the suitcase, and its contents.

vents. Using a 10x14 ferrotype plate, you should be able to peel off three 5x7 prints every five minutes or so at moderate heat (below 150° F).

Keep your equipment to a minimum; any inconvenience resulting from that is outweighed by the convenience of being able to carry everything. Trays do double duty as containers for paper. The enlarger head is cushioned well with foam rubber. Chemicals are all 16-oz. sizes or smaller in powder or concentrate form whenever possible.

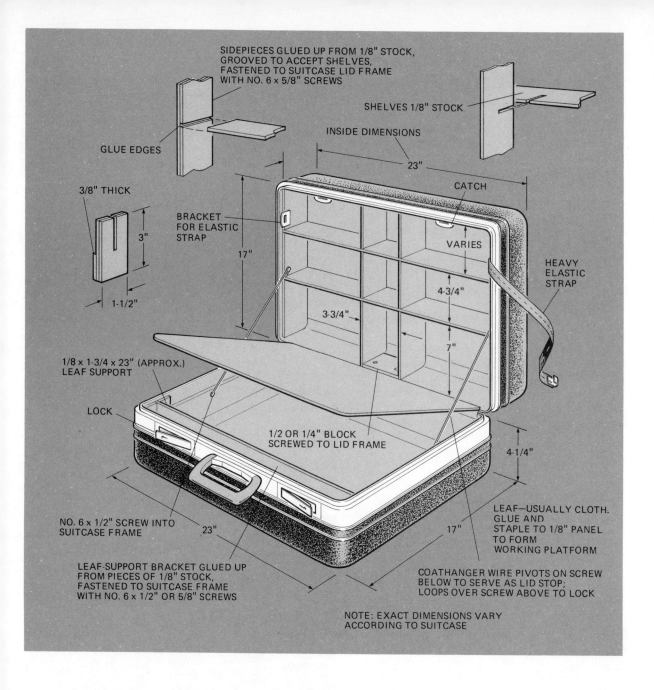

SIDEPIECES GLUED UP FROM 1/8" STOCK, GROOVED TO ACCEPT SHELVES, FASTENED TO SUITCASE LID FRAME WITH NO. 6 x 5/8" SCREWS

SHELVES 1/8" STOCK

GLUE EDGES

INSIDE DIMENSIONS

23"

CATCH

3/8" THICK

BRACKET FOR ELASTIC STRAP

VARIES

3"

17"

HEAVY ELASTIC STRAP

4-3/4"

1-1/2"

3-3/4"

7"

1/8 x 1-3/4 x 23" (APPROX.) LEAF SUPPORT

LOCK

1/2 OR 1/4" BLOCK SCREWED TO LID FRAME

4-1/4"

NO. 6 x 1/2" SCREW INTO SUITCASE FRAME

23"

17"

LEAF—USUALLY CLOTH. GLUE AND STAPLE TO 1/8" PANEL TO FORM WORKING PLATFORM

LEAF-SUPPORT BRACKET GLUED UP FROM PIECES OF 1/8" STOCK, FASTENED TO SUITCASE FRAME WITH NO. 6 x 1/2" OR 5/8" SCREWS

COATHANGER WIRE PIVOTS ON SCREW BELOW TO SERVE AS LID STOP; LOOPS OVER SCREW ABOVE TO LOCK

NOTE: EXACT DIMENSIONS VARY ACCORDING TO SUITCASE

Since you can't always buy the film you want at the prices you're used to, and since some countries limit the number of rolls of film you can take in with you, you can pack a bulk-loader, spare cartridges and film in the long rolls of 27½-100 ft. (at about half the cost of the same film already loaded into cartridges). You should also pack a changing bag, useful not only for loading the bulk-loader and developing tank, but for removing broken or jammed film from a camera without exposing it.

Of course your suitcase holds only a darkroom setup, not the darkroom. But the changing bag takes care of anything that requires *absolute* darkness, and with blankets over the windows and paper stuffed under the door, any room can be an adequate darkroom for printing. You can even do it on an outdoor picnic table after dark.

To keep things from rattling around, the lid of the suitcase is divided into custom-fitted compartments by partitions of ⅛-in. plywood or hardboard, with a fold-down leaf keeping everything in place when you open the lid. The larger items are crammed tightly into the bottom of the suitcase; insulate anything that rattles with spare socks or other clothing items.

Decks and patios you can build

■ DECKS AND PATIOS are fairly easy for a do-it-yourselfer to construct, although patios probably are easier because all the work takes place on the ground. Some deck designs require working from a ladder or scaffolding.

Decks and patios can be any size you want them to be. The standard size is 8 x 10 feet, but consider a larger size if you have the space. The standard size seems to shrink considerably when it becomes filled with furniture and people. In any case, use standard-size building materials; they can save you money and time. For example: 2x8-inch dimension lumber that is often used for deck joists is available in standard lengths of 8, 10, 12, 14, 16, and 20 feet. By designing a deck in any of these modules, you save the time and waste of sawing the 2x8s to a different size.

Decks are more adaptable to homes built on sloping or uneven building lots. Patios are ideal for flat lots. The reason is obvious: It's easier to place concrete, brick, stone, and other materials on flat ground; it's easier to build up and over sloping ground.

Deck and patio design

If you are looking for deck or patio designs to match the architecture of your home, you'll find plenty of ideas in books and magazines. If you have a problem lot, consult an architect or land-

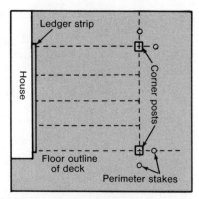

LAY OUT a deck with string and perimeter stakes, which are moved until the structure is square. The corner posts stand where the lines cross. Joists are nailed around the perimeter to the posts and the ledger strip; the space inside the perimeter is filled with joists on 16- or 24-inch centers. Strings can also mark the form placement for patios.

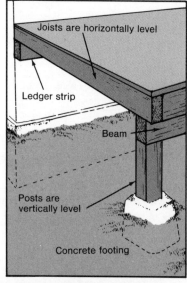

SIDE VIEW of a deck shows how the deck is supported on a ledger strip attached to the house. The support posts must be absolutely plumb (vertically level) to support the superstructure, as well as furniture and people.

scaping architect. The cost of having a deck or patio designed is not as great as you might think. Money you save by building the structure yourself will more than offset any fees, and when the job is completed, you'll have a well-designed deck or patio tailored especially to your needs.

Since deck and patio construction often is subject to local building codes, make sure the structure will conform to the codes *before* you spend any time on design and money on materials. If you intend to light the deck or patio, local electrical codes must be considered. If the area is fenced, you may have to conform to building codes that restrict heights. If the area will include a swimming pool, local codes definitely must be consulted. If your deck will stand more than two or three feet off the ground, consult an architect or engineer for information about the weight and stress loads that will be imposed on the materials you plan to use. If you decide to have a building contractor construct the deck or patio, get at least three bids before signing any contract. It's smart, too, to check the reputation of the contractor you pick with the local Better Business Bureau. Examine some samples of his work and talk to some of his customers. Be sure to get bottom-line costs for the project. Also, set firm completion times and payment dates on any contract.

Deck materials

Decks have several component parts that must be considered before you buy any materials.

Decking is the lumber (2x4s or 2x6s) that forms the floor of the deck. There will be a ⅜-inch space between decking pieces to permit drainage; allow for this measurement in lumber calculations.

The best woods to buy for decking are redwood, cedar, and cypress. These woods will not rot or decay; they never need finishing or refinishing. The second decking choice is pressure-treated lumber—usually structural lumber, such as fir, spruce, and hemlock. The third choice is

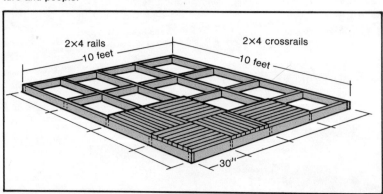

GROUND LEVEL deck is made with an egg-crate framework over which decking is nailed. The frame can sit on concrete footings or concrete blocks.

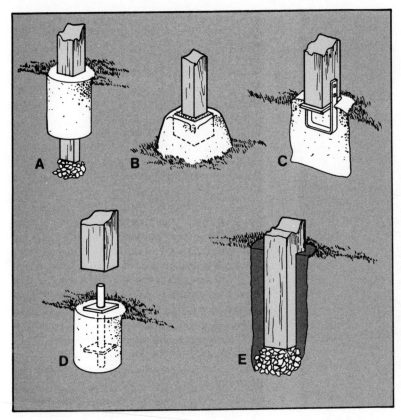

DECK FOOTING construction types include: (A) The post runs through a concrete collar and sits on a bed of gravel for drainage. (B) A wood nailing block is inserted into a block of wet concrete. The post is nailed to the block after the concrete sets. (C) A post anchor is inserted into the wet concrete; the post is bolted to the anchor. (D) A drift pin, made of a piece of heavy reinforcing rod and two metal plates, is inserted into wet concrete. The bottom of the post is drilled to fit over the pin, which prevents the post from drifting. (E) Simple post-in-the-hole construction can be used for very light decks. The wood should be treated with wood preservative and set on two inches of gravel for drainage.

untreated lumber, such as fir, spruce, and hemlock, but this material should be coated with a quality wood preservative before it is put into place.

Joists support the decking; they may be 2x6s, 2x8s, and 2x10s in redwood, cedar, cypress, fir, spruce, and hemlock, or almost any grade of construction lumber. Sizes larger than those mentioned seldom are used since the superstructure of the deck doesn't need any greater support. The spacing of joists is critical to provide support for the live weight loads.

Ledger strips are 2x6s or 2x8s nailed or bolted to the house joists, or attached to masonry with masonry bolts. They support the deck joists.

Beams support the joists and transfer the weight load to the support posts. Wood types can be the same as those mentioned for joists.

Posts support the decking, joists, and beams. Standard 3x4-inch posts may be used for light- to medium-heavy superstructures. For heavy superstructures, timber-type posts are needed.

Footings are supports or the foundation for the entire deck structure. The footings go into the earth and are usually reinforced concrete. Sometimes concrete blocks are used to support a lightweight deck structure. The footings should be

placed below the frost depth; you can find out the frost depth by phoning the National Weather Service in your area. A standard depth is from 36 to 42 inches in most sections of the country; it may be less in the south, southeast, and southwest, where heavy freezing is not commonplace.

Deck height

The base point is the doorway through which people will walk out onto the decking. Therefore, the deck should be the same height as the floor in the house or an easy step down—one to five inches—from the threshold of the door.

When you determine this height, make a mark on the house exactly at the top surface of the decking. You will use this mark to estimate the materials you need.

For slightly raised decks at ground level, you can place the joists directly on the footings. Posts and beams are not needed for this deck design.

Deck fasteners

All framing members should be fastened with galvanized steel carriage bolts and washers, or with lagbolts and washers. The size of the lumber

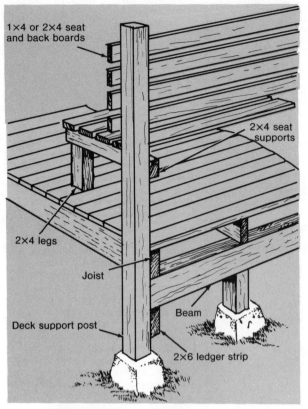

1×4 or 2×4 seat and back boards

2×4 seat supports

2×4 legs

Joist

Deck support post

Beam

2×6 ledger strip

DECK BENCHES are built on support posts. The seat support should be fastened to the post with a lag or carriage bolt; other bench parts are nailed with galvanized or aluminum nails. Beam and ledger construction supports decking.

will determine the size of the fasteners.

Decking should be fastened to joists with either galvanized or coated nails, or with aluminum nails. If you use aluminum nails, drill pilot holes; aluminum nails bend very easily.

The joists may be suspended from any ledger strips with galvanized joist hangers. The hangers will provide more strength and support than bolt assembly or toenailing the joists to the ledge strips.

Footings

Footings are easy to place; simply dig a hole below frost depth and fill it with concrete. Standard footings are 15x15 inches, or 12 inches in diameter. The concrete should be reinforced with ½-inch steel reinforcing rods placed vertically one inch in from the perimeter of the concrete, and in the center of it. If post anchors will be used for support, the anchors are placed in the top of the footing before the concrete hardens.

You have some margin for error when placing the anchors, but they should be centered and level.

Railings, seats, and steps

These components should be considered as part of the design, instead of being added later. This will save you money and time.

Railings, seats, and benches are usually built on the post supports that extend up beyond the decking. The additional support pieces are made from the same materials used for decking and the posts, if the posts are 4x4s.

Posts and other framing can be supported by special hangers and brackets.

Spindles for railings may be metal, lengths of 2x4s spaced at two-foot intervals, or wrought iron railings that are available in kits. The railings themselves can be 2x4s or 2x6s of the same wood as used for the decking and joists.

Benches are built with 4x4s for legs and 2x4s or 2x6s for the seat. Fasteners are countersunk and the holes filled with matching wood filler.

Steps may be cut from 2x12s. Construction is easier if you buy precut step stringers, or carriages, which are available in two-, three-, four-, and five-step increments. The step treads can also be made of 2x4s or 2x6s; nail the treads to the stringers with hot-dipped galvanized or aluminum nails, both of which deter rust and corrosion.

Deck finishes

If the deck is constructed of redwood, cedar, or cypress, the wood does not have to be finished to protect it from the weather, although it may be finished if you wish. But if it is finished, the wood must be maintained by refinishing every three to five years.

A good finish for redwood, cypress, or cedar is a clear penetrating stain; this protects the wood but leaves a natural appearance. If the wood is fir, hemlock, or spruce, use a pigmented penetrating stain. It will color the wood slightly while protecting it from the elements. Stain is also available in colors.

Porch and deck enamel may also be used. It is available in gray, green, and maroon. The enamel actually is a pigmented varnish, and the surfaces have to be refinished every three to five years. Clear spar varnish makes an excellent finish.

Under no circumstances should a deck be painted with standard house paint. This product does not provide a surface hard enough for the heavy foot traffic a deck endures.

Open deck to enjoy the outdoors

■ A WOOD DECK is simply a handsome platform on or above the ground. But it's a platform that adds much to the livability, beauty and value of a house.

A well designed deck can turn a hilly site into a useful, enjoyable outdoor living area at a fraction of the cost of adding an inside room. And there's no substitute for the style of living it can provide as an area for sunbathing, entertaining, dining, conversation, container gardening, children's play and parties.

As an aesthetic assist, good deck design eases the transition from house to garden and is a part of each. Where the land slopes upward from the house, the deck bridges the space with a usable level floor. Where the land slopes down and away, the deck extends the floor of the building out into otherwise wasted space.

Even on land that is generally flat, the deck can be a floor-level area gently leading to the garden a step or two below. Where paving of a flat area may be a practical expedient, a ground-level deck is often preferred for its resilient comfort and drainage advantages. For whatever reasons a deck is desired, it can also be counted on to add permanently to the value of a house as well as enhance its sale appeal.

Lumber selection for the various parts of the deck is based on its function. Thus, supporting elements are picked for strength, members visible to the eye for looks. Douglas fir or kiln-dried hemlock are good choices for beams, joists and the like. Or, if the advantages of redwood's natural resistance to weather are desired, a heartwood grade should be used. The decking, usually 2x4s on the flat, can be fir if it is to be painted, with redwood preferable if it is to remain natural.

Redwood can vary. In addition to the heartwood, there are clear all-heart, select-heart and construction-heart. A-grade, sap-common and merchantable grades permit the presence of some cream-colored sapwood. (*Note:* Sapwood is not decay-resistant and should only be used above ground.) If redwood is your choice for decking, you can use either clear all-heart or construction-heart, depending upon the appearance you desire.

The general approach to laying out a deck is to first decide on its size and then choose a pattern. Next, select the grade material you plan to use and determine the joist layout. With sketch in hand, visit your local building department. Someone will advise you about the size materials you will need for the structural members—posts, beams and joists.

• *Decking:* The deck surface—size, lumber grade and design—determines the arrangement and size of the framing. Two-inch (nominal) redwood (or fir if deck will be painted) is recommended for most decking situations. You'll find 2x4s and 2x6s are the most common sizes and minimize chance of cupping. Nominal 1-in.-

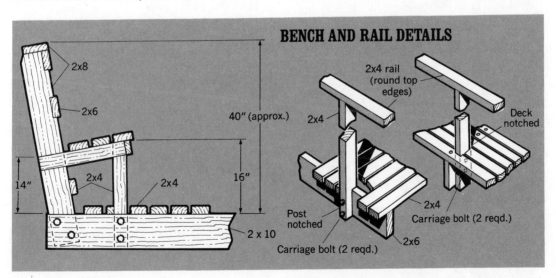

BENCH AND RAIL DETAILS

2x8

2x6

40" (approx.)

16"

14"

2x4

2x4

2 x 10

2x4 rail (round top edges)

2x4

Deck notched

Post notched

Carriage bolt (2 reqd.)

2x4

Carriage bolt (2 reqd.)

2x6

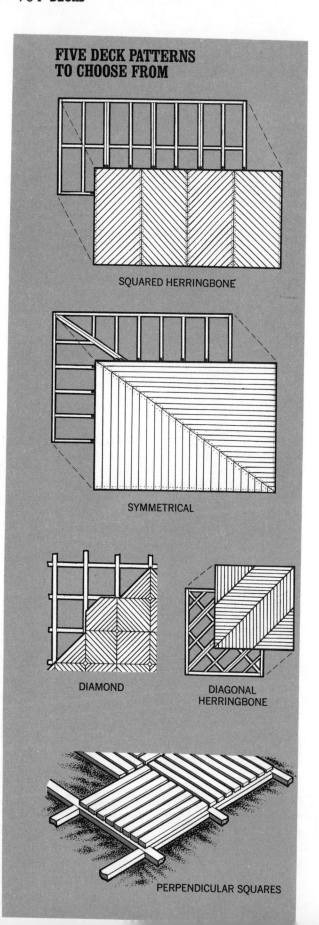

FIVE DECK PATTERNS TO CHOOSE FROM

SQUARED HERRINGBONE

SYMMETRICAL

DIAMOND

DIAGONAL HERRINGBONE

PERPENDICULAR SQUARES

thick material may be used where joists are 16 in. o.c. or less. If a pattern of narrow lines is desired, use 2x4s on edge.

● *Joists:* Joists (usually 2-in. dimension lumber) bear the load of the decking and whatever loads are imposed upon it. It follows that the longer the distance a joist must span, the larger the joist must be to prevent sagging.

Joists usually rest upon a beam or are fastened to a header. If they must not rise higher than the beam, they may be hung from the beam by a patented joist hanger or fastened to the beam using a ledger strip nailed to the joist. The joists can overhang (cantilever) slightly beyond (outside) the beam for appearance or added size if desired. Overhang limit depends upon width of the joist and should in no case exceed ¼ of the joist's length. Bridging is usually installed at mid-span to strengthen joists.

● *Beams:* Beams rest upon the posts and support the joists. The size required depends upon the weight that will be imposed. However, a general rule is to utilize as large a beam as necessary in order to minimize the number of posts and footings. Beams of 4-in. thickness and greater are often used, and since these thicker members are not always readily available, it is sometimes necessary to construct a "built-up" beam by spiking thinner members together.

The beam can be fastened to post tops by a metal post-connector or a wooden cleat bolted or nailed to the post and beam. When the post must extend above the deck level to support a railing, seat or overhead shelter, the joists may be supported on paired members bolted to the posts. When the beam rests directly on footings, it should be anchored to the footings with nailing blocks or anchor bolts.

Where length of the deck requires splicing a beam, make butt joints over supporting posts and tie two beams together with cleats on each side.

● *Ledgers:* When deck height is of concern, joists can be supported by a ledger strip attached to the house or beam. Care should be taken to insure full bearing on the ledger strip. To prevent rain or snow from wetting interior floors the ledger should be located so that deck surface is at least 1 in. below the house floor.

● *Posts:* The posts bear the weight of the deck, transmitting it through the footings to the ground. For most low decks, the 4x4 is an adequate post. For steep sites, or for heavy loads such as large groups of people, snow, or plant containers, larger posts will be required to bear the weight.

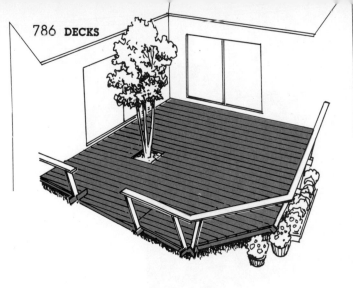

corners or across the understructure may be the only way to achieve the stability required by local building regulations.

● *Footings:* The footing anchors the entire structure and transmits the weight of the deck to the ground. Building codes are specific on the subject of footings. Generally, they must extend to undisturbed soil or rock and, in cold climates, must be below the frost line (local codes determine depth). If concrete footings are site-poured, metal post-anchors or steel straps may be set in the wet concrete. Drift pins offer a concealed method of connecting the post to the footing when the underside of the deck is to be in open view. While anchors of metal are the most rigid and are recommended for high decks, wood nailing blocks imbedded in concrete usually are adequate for low decks.

Locations and placement of footings are determined by the design of the deck's structural members so that weight is properly transmitted to the ground. Placement points can be ascertained with a tape measure, a string, or a long, straight 2x4 and a wooden peg.

If the deck is to extend from a corner of the house, you can simply project a straight line from the nondeck side of the house out to where one corner of the deck will extend. Then measure and mark the points within the line where footings will be needed.

Where a beam bears upon the top of a post, the length of the post must be carefully measured and trimmed to insure solid bearing for the beam. Accurate measurement may be achieved by carefully leveling the beam from a reference elevation on the house. Mark the level position, adjust for slope of deck, if any, and trim carefully. The post should be plumb when measured and installed.

Cross bracing may be necessary to prevent lateral movement of the deck, particularly if it is elevated high above the ground. Good connections between post and beam will help brace the deck structure, but diagonal bracing across

FLOOR AND RAIL CONSTRUCTION

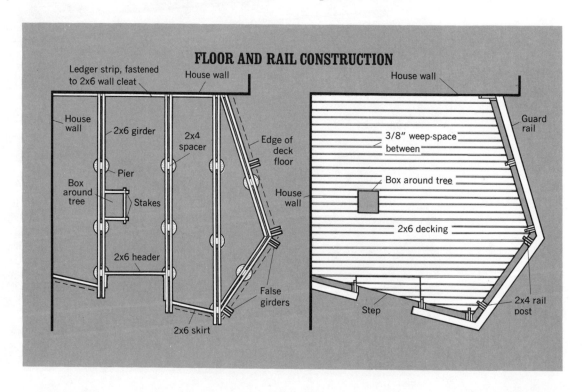

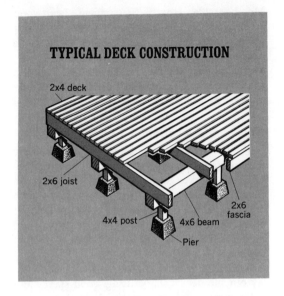

TYPICAL DECK CONSTRUCTION

2x4 deck

2x6 joist

4x4 post

4x6 beam

2x6 fascia

Pier

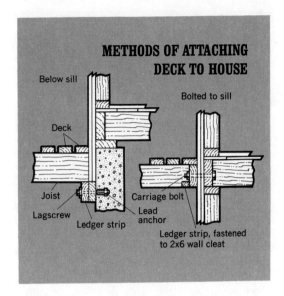

METHODS OF ATTACHING DECK TO HOUSE

Below sill

Bolted to sill

Deck

Joist

Lagscrew

Ledger strip

Carriage bolt

Lead anchor

Ledger strip, fastened to 2x6 wall cleat

With this right angle (consisting of the line and the deck side of the house) established, two corners of the deck are determined. The length of the deck is then measured along the wall from the corner of the house. With a third corner thus established, location of the other corner footing can easily be fixed with tape measurement from these established points.

Accuracy of the four points can be proven by diagonal measurements between the farthest corners. If these diagonal distances are at variance, the deck is not square. This could be the fault of either an out-of-square house or inaccurate measurement. If the former, design the deck to match the house.

Here is another way to place footings:

If the deck is to project from a wall where a corner line projection is not convenient, a right-angle projection can be made by creating a mathematical right-angle triangle of 6x8x10 ft. or proportionally larger. This is done by marking a point (A) on the house wall which designates one corner of the deck. Measure 6 ft. from point A one way on the wall to establish point B. To establish the right angle desired between point A and C (8 ft.), the mathematical triangle which establishes this right angle can be created using a taut string approximately 2 ft. longer than the outside dimension of the deck. This string, nailed to a "batter board," should be pulled out from the wall. Then a long 2x4 marked at 10 ft. can be extended from point B to point C. The string and the marked 2x4 may have to be moved left or right until the marks on each match. When they do, a right angle has been created to use as

a reference point for placement of footings where desired inside or outside the triangle. Other footings can be placed by measurements from this reference point and the wall reference points.

Lay out decking on the joists so that any butt joints that may occur are at random intervals and over joists. Joints should never occur on adjacent pieces of decking unless the pattern dictates. It is better to trim decking to size as it is used, rather than trimming first, in order to fit to any variations caused by installation of the framing or other decking. When decking is laid parallel to the house, make sure the first piece is properly aligned both with the house and at the proper angle to the joists.

Vertical-grain lumber is recommended for decking, but when flat-grained lumber is used it is important to make sure that the bark side of the piece is up. Either side of a vertical grain piece may be up when the piece is laid.

● *Nails:* Use only corrosion-resistant nails for secure holding power and to avoid rust stains on the wood. Stainless steel and aluminum never cause staining. If these are not locally available, hot-dipped, high-quality galvanized nails with a ring or spiral shank are adequate. For 2-in. decking, use 16d nails; for 1-in. decking, 8d.

● *Nailing:* Predrill holes for nails at the ends of decking pieces to avoid splitting. Seasoned decking material should be spaced a minimum of ⅛ in. apart for water drainage. Use only one nail per bearing, alternating from one side of the piece to the other. The nailing on alternate sides overcomes any tendency to pull or cup. Keep nails in alignment for best appearance.

Deck for anywhere

■ AS PROPERTY VALUES continue to rise and building lots shrink, many homeowners are searching for ways to develop additional living space. One of the most popular and economical methods is to build a wood deck attached to the house. This extends interior space for eating, playing, working and entertaining.

The deck shown here offers all the benefits of a house-attached deck with one unique difference—the freedom to be built independent of another structure. Its free-standing design means it can be placed near a garden or lake, at poolside, under shady trees, or on sloping, rocky or otherwise unmanageable terrain.

Construction and materials notes

The deck's size and shape can be altered to suit your particular site, but the basic structural design can be used in any situation. Be sure to check the local building codes before you begin construction.

This deck was built to extend beyond an existing concrete patio to afford views of the picturesque canyon below. It's made of construction heart redwood that is used for outdoor applications.

Redwood was chosen for more than its looks. It's also dimensionally stable, so it resists warping, cupping and checking; it is lightweight and easy to work with; and redwood heartwood resists insects and decay. Redwood readily holds a finish and doesn't burn easily because it contains no volatile substances.

Use only redwood heartwood or pressure-treated lumber in or near the ground. Redwood sapwood is not decay-resistant.

Garden grades of redwood

Construction Heart: All heartwood, but does contain some knots. Suitable for posts, beams and structural framing near or on the ground.
Construction Common: Similar to construction heart, but contains sapwood. For use as deck boards, fences and other above-ground applications.

Merchantable Heart: Economical heartwood grade with larger knots and holes. Used for fences, garden structures and other applications at or near the ground.
Merchantable: Same as merchantable heart, but contains sapwood. Suitable for trellises, deck furnishings and other above-ground uses.

Choosing a location

The first step is to pick a spot on your property to build the deck. This decision is important because it's the key to the deck's usefulness. When choosing a site, consider the following: the path of the sun, water drainage patterns, the amount of available shade, privacy from neighbors and traffic, access to the house, and protection from wind and noise.

Next, to help you visualize the completed deck, lay out the deck's shape using wood stakes and nylon string. The deck size and shape are most often determined by the site's terrain and your budget. But remember, even a modest-size deck like the one shown provides over 250 sq. ft. of extra living space.

Time-saving galvanized metal fasteners are used throughout the deck construction to join structural wood members. Fasteners are available at lumberyards, home centers and hardwood stores. Refer to drawings for the specific model Teco fasteners used.

Footings and piers

Footings, generally made of poured concrete, support the posts that transfer the weight of the entire deck to the ground. A concrete pier is often poured on top of the footing to raise the post off the ground (see drawing of typical footings). Generally, footings measure 8 in. deep x 16 x 16 in.

Pour the footings onto undisturbed or well-compacted soil or rock, not loose backfill. In colder regions, dig footings below the frost line to avoid heaving during freeze and thaw cycles. Check the local building code for specific footing size and depth in your area.

Lay out and dig the 12 footings as shown in the plan. Next, decide whether you want to use ready-mixed concrete or mix your own from cement, sand, gravel and water. Ready-mixed concrete costs more, but you only need to add water and mix.

If a pier is to be poured on top of the footing, be sure to leave three or four short reinforcing bars (rebars) protruding out of the footing about 6 in. to create a strong bond between the pier and

PLAN VIEW

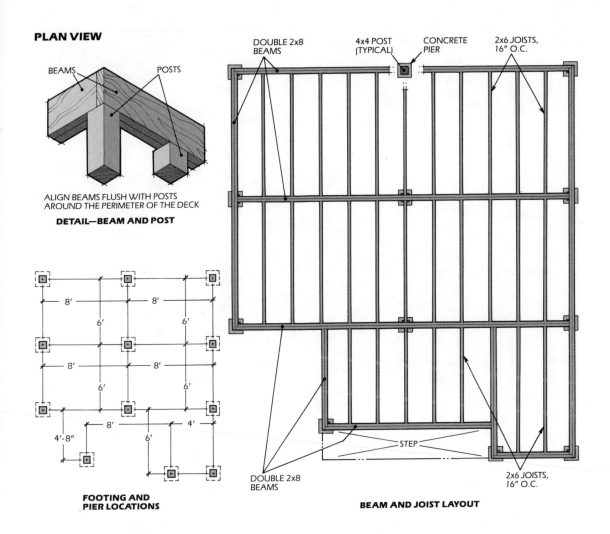

BEAMS
POSTS

ALIGN BEAMS FLUSH WITH POSTS
AROUND THE PERIMETER OF THE DECK

DETAIL—BEAM AND POST

DOUBLE 2x8
BEAMS

4x4 POST
(TYPICAL)

CONCRETE
PIER

2x6 JOISTS,
16" O.C.

8'   8'
6'   6'
8'   8'
6'   6'
8'   4'
4'-8'   6'

**FOOTING AND
PIER LOCATIONS**

DOUBLE 2x8
BEAMS

STEP

2x6 JOISTS,
16" O.C.

BEAM AND JOIST LAYOUT

TYPICAL FOOTING CONSTRUCTION

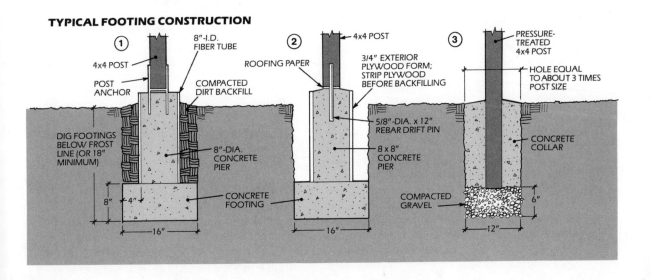

①

4x4 POST

POST
ANCHOR

8"-I.D.
FIBER TUBE

COMPACTED
DIRT BACKFILL

DIG FOOTINGS
BELOW FROST
LINE (OR 18"
MINIMUM)

8"-DIA.
CONCRETE
PIER

8"   4"

16"

CONCRETE
FOOTING

②

4x4 POST

ROOFING PAPER

3/4" EXTERIOR
PLYWOOD FORM;
STRIP PLYWOOD
BEFORE BACKFILLING

5/8"-DIA. x 12"
REBAR DRIFT PIN

8 x 8"
CONCRETE
PIER

16"

③

PRESSURE-
TREATED
4x4 POST

HOLE EQUAL
TO ABOUT 3 TIMES
POST SIZE

CONCRETE
COLLAR

COMPACTED
GRAVEL

12"   6"

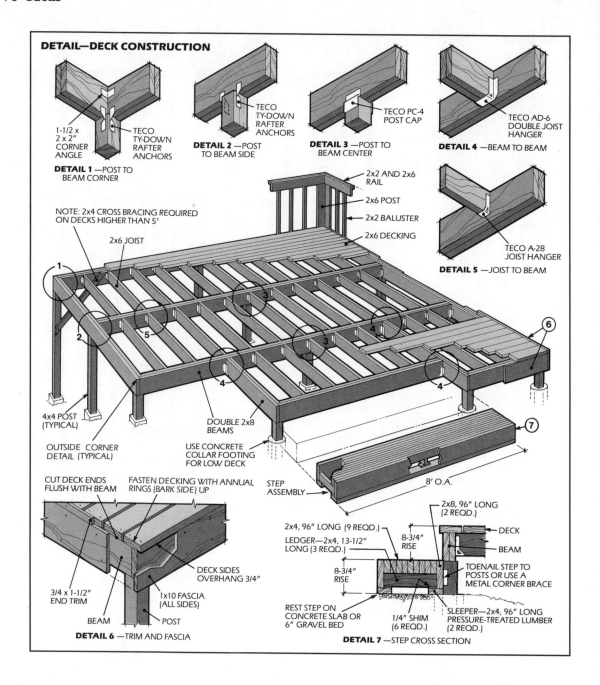

DETAIL—DECK CONSTRUCTION

1-1/2 x 2 x 2" CORNER ANGLE

TECO TY-DOWN RAFTER ANCHORS

DETAIL 1—POST TO BEAM CORNER

TECO TY-DOWN RAFTER ANCHORS

DETAIL 2—POST TO BEAM SIDE

TECO PC-4 POST CAP

DETAIL 3—POST TO BEAM CENTER

TECO AD-6 DOUBLE JOIST HANGER

DETAIL 4—BEAM TO BEAM

TECO A-28 JOIST HANGER

DETAIL 5—JOIST TO BEAM

2x2 AND 2x6 RAIL

2x6 POST

2x2 BALUSTER

2x6 DECKING

NOTE: 2x4 CROSS BRACING REQUIRED ON DECKS HIGHER THAN 5'

2x6 JOIST

4x4 POST (TYPICAL)

OUTSIDE CORNER DETAIL (TYPICAL)

DOUBLE 2x8 BEAMS

USE CONCRETE COLLAR FOOTING FOR LOW DECK

STEP ASSEMBLY

8' O.A.

CUT DECK ENDS FLUSH WITH BEAM

FASTEN DECKING WITH ANNUAL RINGS (BARK SIDE) UP

DECK SIDES OVERHANG 3/4"

3/4 x 1-1/2" END TRIM

1x10 FASCIA (ALL SIDES)

BEAM

POST

DETAIL 6—TRIM AND FASCIA

2x8, 96" LONG (2 REQD.)

DECK

BEAM

2x4, 96" LONG (9 REQD.)

LEDGER—2x4, 13-1/2" LONG (3 REQD.)

8-3/4" RISE

8-3/4" RISE

TOENAIL STEP TO POSTS OR USE A METAL CORNER BRACE

REST STEP ON CONCRETE SLAB OR 6" GRAVEL BED

1/4" SHIM (6 REQD.)

SLEEPER—2x4, 96" LONG PRESSURE-TREATED LUMBER (2 REQD.)

DETAIL 7—STEP CROSS SECTION

the footing. After the footing has hardened, you can form up and pour the pier.

Build the pier's form using ¾-in. exterior plywood or an 8-in.-dia. spiral-wound fiber tube. The tube, commonly known by the trade name Sonotube, is a thick-walled paper tube designed for use as a concrete form. Piers should be at least 8 in. wide and project above the ground a minimum of 6 in. If a drift pin or metal post anchor is to be used, be sure to insert it into the pier before

the concrete hardens. Cut the pin from a length of ⅝- or ¾-in.-dia. rebar. Then centerbore the bottom of the post to accept the pin.

Posts and beams

First, cut the 4 x 4 posts slightly longer than needed, then position each post on its pier. If a drift pin is used, place a 4 x 4-in. square of heavy roofing paper over the pin to prevent the post from absorbing moisture. Brace each post temporarily with 1 x 3s. Use a carpenter's level to be sure each post is plumb.

Next, determine the posts' finished height by subtracting the decking thickness and the beam width from the desired finished deck height. For example, if the finished deck height is 30 in., subtract the 2 x 6 decking (1½ in. thick) and the 2 x 8 beam (7¼ in. wide) to arrive at a post height of 21¼ in.

Mark the post height onto the post that is sitting on the highest point of ground. From here, transfer the post height to the other posts using a nylon string and a line level. Then carefully mark and cut each post where indicated by the level string.

At this point, the posts may be different lengths because of sloping or uneven terrain, but the tops of all the posts should be level with each other.

Nail together the double 2 x 8 beams using 3-in. (10d) top-quality, double hot-dipped galvanized nails. The beam ends that meet to form the outside corners are assembled with the inside 2 x 8 held back 1½ in. in order to form a strong interlocking corner joint.

Next, get the metal fasteners ready to use. Use two Ty-down rafter anchors on each of the 10 posts located around the deck perimeter (details 1 and 2). Fasten one angle-iron brace in each corner to further strengthen the joint.

On the two posts located in the center of the deck, use a Teco No. PC-4 post cap (detail 3). For the six places where a beam meets a beam, excluding the outside corners, use a 3-in.-wide double-joist hanger (detail 4).

With the aid of a helper, lift one of the perimeter deck beams onto the posts. Fasten the rafter anchors to the beam first. Then position the beam flush with the outside of the posts and nail the anchors to the posts. Continue nailing the beams in place to form the deck perimeter. Install the two beams that cross the center posts. Use a double-joist hanger (detail 4) where a center beam meets a perimeter beam.

Joists

Mark 16-in. on-center locations for all the 2 x 6 joist hangers (detail 5). Next, nail the hangers in place, but fasten only *one* side of each hanger. Then cut the joists and drop them into the hangers. Before nailing the joists in place, sight down the joist edge. If a noticeable crown (crook) exists, position the joist with the crowned edge up. The weight of the deck will straighten the joist. Finish nailing the hangers. For single-joist hangers, use 3-in. (10d) nails. Use 4-in. (20d) nails for double-joist hangers.

Bracing

Braces are required on decks higher than 5 ft. to prevent lateral movement. Bolt the braces to the underside of the deck, as shown, using ¼-in.-dia. x 6-in. carriage bolts.

Decking

Starting at the back of the deck, nail down the first 2 x 6 deck board using 3½-in. (16d) galvanized nails. Let the board edge overhang the beam ¾ in. to conceal the fascia (see detail 6). Start with a straight board since measurements taken from here are used to keep subsequent boards straight.

If more than one board is used to span the deck, butt the boards over the center of a joist. Be sure to stagger the next row of boards to prevent the joint from falling on the same joist as the previous row. Also, leave space for expansion and drainage. The shank of a 16d nail is commonly used as a spacer. You can also use a block of ¼-in. plywood.

As you nail each row, let the board ends overhang the sides of the deck. Later, snap a chalkline and trim all the boards using a portable circular saw.

After every five or six rows, stop and take measurements from the starter board. If the boards are out of alignment, make several small adjustments to consecutive rows rather than one large adjustment. When you reach the final board, let it overhang the front edge of the deck ¾ in. As with the first board, this will conceal the fascia.

Next, snap a chalkline on both sides of the deck flush with the outside edge of the beam. Then trim off the board ends using a portable circular saw. *Caution:* Be certain to wear eye protection when operating any power tool.

Build the butcher block step as shown in detail 7. Fasten the step assembly to the posts using metal corner braces or by toenailing.

Finishes

A clear water repellent containing a mildewcide should be applied to all garden-grade redwood. For best results, apply the water repellent directly to the lumber before construction, covering all surfaces. Then apply a second coat after the deck is completed.

If water repellent is applied every 12 to 18 months, it will eliminate the natural darkening process and help stabilize the color of the redwood to a buckskin tan. Water repellent also serves as a base for other finishes such as exterior oil-based decking stains.

Deck ideas you can borrow

■ OUTDOOR-LIVING has become a way of life for the typical American family. Moderate seasons and temperate climates especially stimulate the desire for an "outdoor family room." The cost to build a deck is substantially lower than that of a same-size addition and, considering the use that the entire family will get from the new space. It's money well spent.

We've rounded up some particularly handsome decks—including the double-tiered variety for hilly sites. In addition, you'll find all the basics you need to know for good deck

DECKS ARE OFTEN the only means for outdoor living on steep building plots and are popular for homes on level ground as well. The house-coordinated deck plays an important role; it provides an adult entertainment center at night and a play area for the children by day.

THIS HUGE double-tiered deck extends along the entire length of the house at the rear.

TYPICAL PATIO CONSTRUCTION

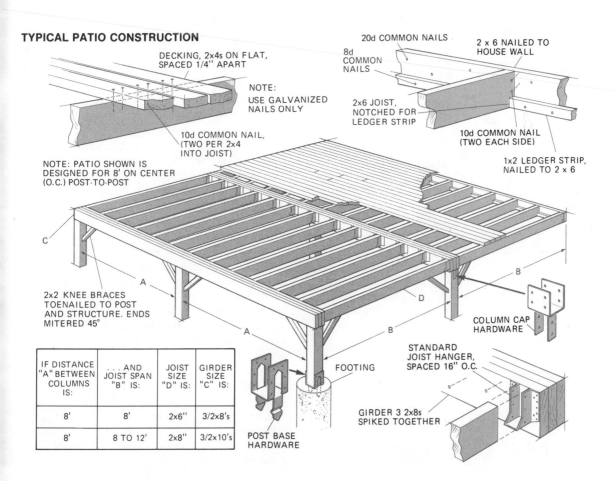

DECKING, 2x4s ON FLAT, SPACED 1/4" APART

NOTE: USE GALVANIZED NAILS ONLY

10d COMMON NAIL, (TWO PER 2x4 INTO JOIST)

20d COMMON NAILS

8d COMMON NAILS

2 x 6 NAILED TO HOUSE WALL

2x6 JOIST, NOTCHED FOR LEDGER STRIP

10d COMMON NAIL (TWO EACH SIDE)

1x2 LEDGER STRIP, NAILED TO 2 x 6

NOTE: PATIO SHOWN IS DESIGNED FOR 8' ON CENTER (O.C.) POST-TO-POST

C

A

2x2 KNEE BRACES TOENAILED TO POST AND STRUCTURE. ENDS MITERED 45°

A

B

D

B

COLUMN CAP HARDWARE

FOOTING

STANDARD JOIST HANGER, SPACED 16" O.C.

POST BASE HARDWARE

GIRDER 3 2x8s SPIKED TOGETHER

IF DISTANCE "A" BETWEEN COLUMNS IS:	. . . AND JOIST SPAN "B" IS:	JOIST SIZE "D" IS:	GIRDER SIZE "C" IS:
8'	8'	2x6"	3/2x8's
8'	8 TO 12'	2x8"	3/2x10's

HOW TO LAY OUT STAIRS

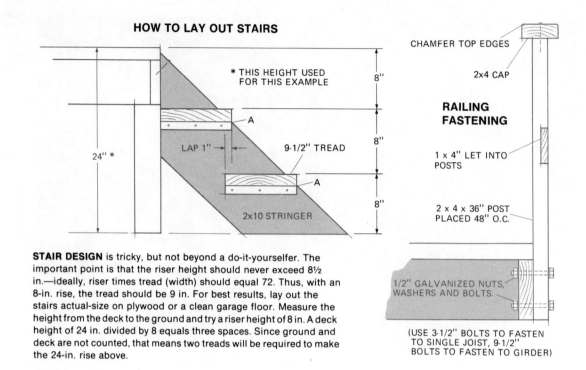

* THIS HEIGHT USED
FOR THIS EXAMPLE

8"

A

8"

LAP 1"

9-1/2" TREAD

24" *

A

8"

2x10 STRINGER

CHAMFER TOP EDGES

2x4 CAP

**RAILING
FASTENING**

1 x 4" LET INTO
POSTS

2 x 4 x 36" POST
PLACED 48" O.C.

1/2" GALVANIZED NUTS,
WASHERS AND BOLTS.

(USE 3-1/2" BOLTS TO FASTEN
TO SINGLE JOIST, 9-1/2"
BOLTS TO FASTEN TO GIRDER)

STAIR DESIGN is tricky, but not beyond a do-it-yourselfer. The important point is that the riser height should never exceed 8½ in.—ideally, riser times tread (width) should equal 72. Thus, with an 8-in. rise, the tread should be 9 in. For best results, lay out the stairs actual-size on plywood or a clean garage floor. Measure the height from the deck to the ground and try a riser height of 8 in. A deck height of 24 in. divided by 8 equals three spaces. Since ground and deck are not counted, that means two treads will be required to make the 24-in. rise above.

**SECTION DRAWING
OF METHOD
FOR FASTENING
TO HOUSE**

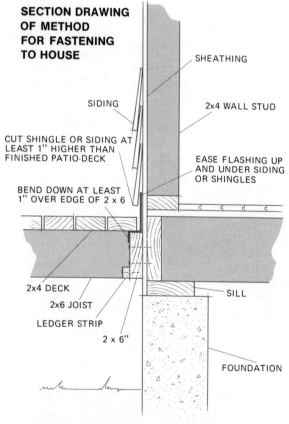

SHEATHING

SIDING

2x4 WALL STUD

CUT SHINGLE OR SIDING AT
LEAST 1" HIGHER THAN
FINISHED PATIO-DECK

EASE FLASHING UP
AND UNDER SIDING
OR SHINGLES

BEND DOWN AT LEAST
1" OVER EDGE OF 2 x 6

2x4 DECK

2x6 JOIST

LEDGER STRIP

2 x 6"

SILL

FOUNDATION

* NOTE: FINISHED PATIO-DECK SHOULD
BE LOWER THAN INTERIOR FLOOR

construction shown in the drawings on these pages. Even if you decide to have a contractor build your deck, the information given in the drawings will let you determine whether the job is being done properly.

The type of materials you use is important. Usual decking requirements are wood that offers a high decay resistance, nonsplintering, good stiffness (for strength), wear resistance and minimal chance of warping. Woods with heartwood that combine these characteristics—from a good to a high degree—include: southern pine, cedar, redwood and cypress.

Open decking, as shown in the sketches, is usually nominal 2x4s spaced ¼ in. apart over joists. Here, because rainwater will run through the deck, good drainage below—away from the house—is a must. For a solid deck, which will be covered by outdoor carpet, use only exterior-grade plywood over the joists. Keep in mind that a solid deck must be pitched to provide positive water runoff. Flashing, installed as shown, is imperative.

Preservation treatment of wood decking is also important in extending the life of the deck. So, if possible, use wood that has been pressure-treated and, for longevity, treat your decks annually with preservative.

Local building codes vary on requirements for decks of this type.

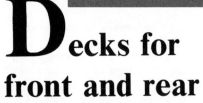

Decks for front and rear

RUGGED REAR DECK on this home is built for years of outdoor living. Perimeter railing incorporates benches to provide ample seating for large gatherings. The front deck was kept simple; the focal point is the group of planting containers along the house wall. The steps are thick wooden slabs.

■ IF YOU HAVE THE SPACE, a well-designed, solidly built deck or patio will add a great deal to your home. Besides improving the looks of many homes, a handsome deck can alter a family's life style during the warm-weather months. And a well-built deck increases a home's value. If it is do-it-yourself built, the investment will probably be returned in full if you decide to sell your house.

The decks shown here made handsome additions to this vacation home. If you are contemplating building a deck, take a drive around your area and see what others have done. Frequently, a good deck design is nothing more than a com-

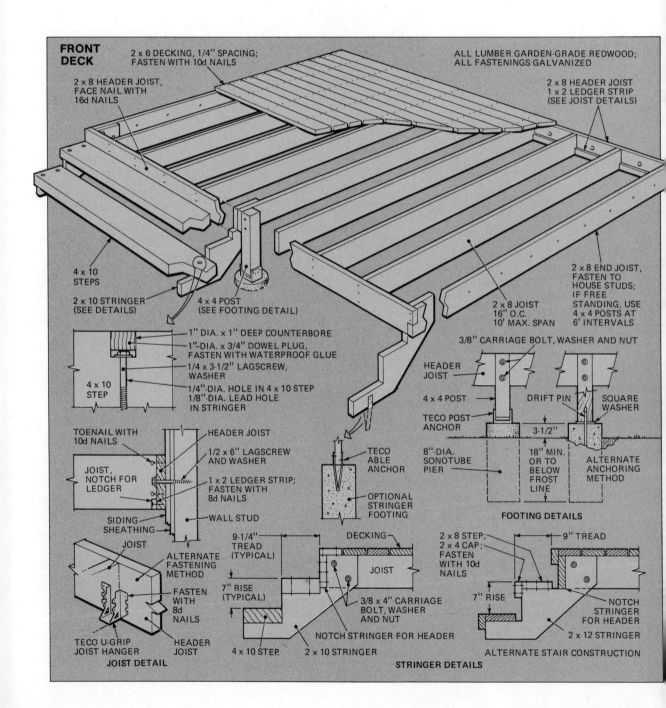

bination of ideas taken from other decks and adapted to your special needs. Use the plans presented here as the starting point for your own design.

For longevity, as well as appearance, be a little choosy about the wood that will make up your patio. You should settle for nothing less than pressure-treated lumber or redwood.

The first is pressure treated to assure many years of resistance to rot and decay, while redwood has a natural resistance to insect infestation. The latter is frequently chosen for use on decks because of its beauty. When treated periodically with the recommended clear preservative, redwood ages to a handsome silver gray patina.

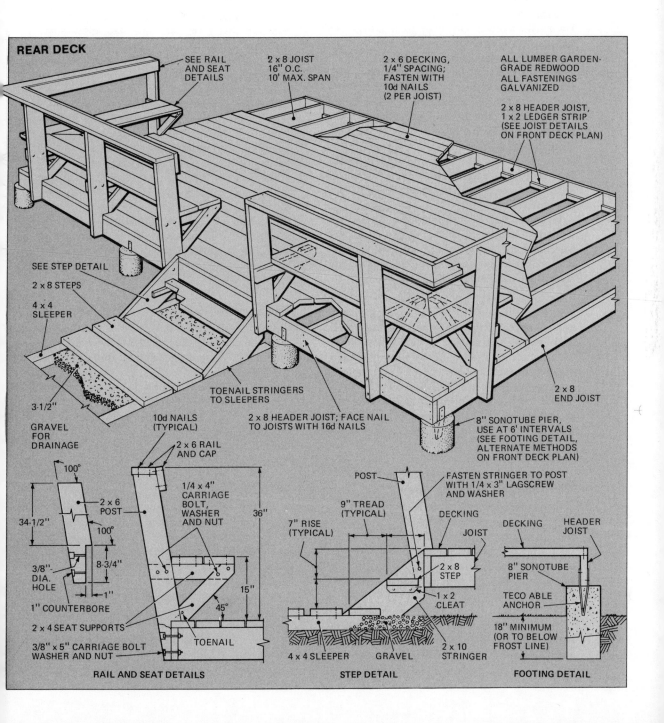

REAR DECK

SEE RAIL AND SEAT DETAILS

2 x 8 JOIST 16" O.C. 10' MAX. SPAN

2 x 6 DECKING, 1/4" SPACING; FASTEN WITH 10d NAILS (2 PER JOIST)

ALL LUMBER GARDEN-GRADE REDWOOD ALL FASTENINGS GALVANIZED

2 x 8 HEADER JOIST, 1 x 2 LEDGER STRIP (SEE JOIST DETAILS ON FRONT DECK PLAN)

SEE STEP DETAIL

2 x 8 STEPS

4 x 4 SLEEPER

3-1/2"

GRAVEL FOR DRAINAGE

10d NAILS (TYPICAL)

2 x 6 RAIL AND CAP

TOENAIL STRINGERS TO SLEEPERS

2 x 8 HEADER JOIST; FACE NAIL TO JOISTS WITH 16d NAILS

2 x 8 END JOIST

8" SONOTUBE PIER, USE AT 6' INTERVALS (SEE FOOTING DETAIL, ALTERNATE METHODS ON FRONT DECK PLAN)

100°

2 x 6 POST

34-1/2"

100°

3/8" DIA. HOLE

8-3/4"

1"

1" COUNTERBORE

2 x 4 SEAT SUPPORTS

3/8" x 5" CARRIAGE BOLT WASHER AND NUT

1/4 x 4" CARRIAGE BOLT, WASHER AND NUT

36"

15"

45°

TOENAIL

RAIL AND SEAT DETAILS

POST

9" TREAD (TYPICAL)

7" RISE (TYPICAL)

FASTEN STRINGER TO POST WITH 1/4 x 3" LAGSCREW AND WASHER

DECKING

JOIST

2 x 8 STEP

1 x 2 CLEAT

4 x 4 SLEEPER   GRAVEL   2 x 10 STRINGER

STEP DETAIL

DECKING

HEADER JOIST

8" SONOTUBE PIER

TECO ABLE ANCHOR

18" MINIMUM (OR TO BELOW FROST LINE)

FOOTING DETAIL

Both types of wood (even the pressure treated, with its slight greenish cast) can be stained to suit the decor you plan for your yard. A sensible lumber choice might be to use pressure-treated material for the understructure—piers, joists, etc.—and redwood for decks and railings.

Planning your deck or patio

It's easiest if you start by sketching your planned deck on ½-in.-scaled graph paper. Though the temptation may be great to make the deck extra large, keep in mind that as its size increases so does the cost to build.

When you are satisfied with your floor plan sketch, move out to the actual job site. Carry along a number of 1x3 wooden stakes, a ball of mason's line, a tape measure and a hand sledge. Using the tape, lay out the perimeter of the deck, using the stakes and mason's line. Check corners for square, using the 6, 8 and 10-ft. method (when one leg of a corner is 6 ft. and the second is 8 ft., the corner is perfectly square when the hypotenuse equals 10 ft.).

When the deck has been staked out, step back and take a long, hard look. If you're dissatisfied with the shape, size or appearance, rearrange the lines until you find a deck shape that seems to be compatible with both house and yard.

Rework your sketch, if necessary, and take it to your local building department to learn if a permit will be required. Local requirements for such decks vary. There may be restrictions on the location of the deck (away from lot lines), the materials to be used, and how the deck is fastened to existing structures. In some cases you will want to exceed local codes. For example, concrete piers are not always required to meet the law, but are a must if your deck is to be well-anchored and last for years.

Deck-building hints and tips

In general, building a deck is a chore well within the skills of the average do-it-yourselfer. But there are exceptions: If yours will be on steeply pitched ground, or well up in the air, you may be well-advised to call in a qualified professional contractor for some assistance in pouring the footings and the like. Hillside construction is tricky, at best.

You can build a deck with mostly hand tools—hammer, saw, square, brace and bit, level, and shovels, but a couple of the right power tools will make the job go faster and save your back. A portable drill and circular saw will save many arm-wearying hours when building a deck.

Since dimensional lumber is the best bet when building a deck, we designed ours to make use of such readily available stock. With the exception of the 4x10 steps on the front deck, all materials are carried by well-stocked lumberyards and home centers. To save frustration and hunting for the 4x10s (such stock may be hard to come by in some areas), we show an alternate step construction that gives the same slab appearance, except that you make the treads using 2x4s and 2x8s. (See detail in lower right-hand corner of drawing.)

There are several ways of fastening a deck to a house. We decided to use the header joist-and-joist-hanger method. The header joist is well secured to the house with hefty lagscrews through siding and into wall studs. (*Note:* Lagscrews *must* be anchored in studs, or the header joist may separate from house wall.) On the model house we used metal hangers to secure joists to header joists; but you can avoid buying the connectors by fastening ledger strips to header joists as shown in the drawing. In this case, every joist should be carefully notched to assure its seating squarely on the ledger strip.

Use rustproof hardware

You do not need a great deal of hardware to build either deck. So spend a couple of more bucks and buy only galvanized hardware. It is worth the extra cost to avoid the rust stains that will appear if you use ordinary steel hardware and expose it to the weather. And, do take time to bore pilot holes for nails when fastening near the end of a board; this will prevent splits in your expensive lumber.

About the deck floor

The deck floor is the most visible part of your deck. Take your time when installing the floor to make certain it will have a craftsman-like appearance. Our pattern is a simple one—the same-width deck boards are laid parallel with ends staggered over various joists. You may opt for a herringbone design, or experiment with alternate widths to come up with a look of your own choosing. No matter which pattern you elect to use on your deck, make it a point to lay each board with its bark side up.

Floor plan labels: LOWER DECK · 42" HIGH COUNTER · 3 x 8' BUILT-IN TABLE · STEPS DOWN · RAILROAD TIE · EXISTING GROUND PLANTING · 36" HIGH RAILING · BUILT-IN SEATING · PICNIC TABLE AND BENCH AREA · 10 x 20' UPPER DECK · SLIDING DOORS · GAS-FIRED BARBECUE · RAISED PLANTER · 34" HIGH COUNTER · 36" HIGH RAILING

FLOOR PLAN (above, left) shows the well-thought-out layout. Access to the house and kitchen is through the sliding glass doors to the family room.

Decks on two levels for entertaining

■ THIS UNIQUE DECK is loaded with special features:

● The deck is a multilevel one which, in effect, makes the upper level an outdoor continuation of the family room. A pair of sliding doors is located between the two.

● The deck's two levels automatically separate activities; there is a comfortable place for those who want to pursue quiet activities on the upper level, while the lower level is fully exposed to the sun for sunbathing, entertaining, or just plain fun and games.

● Deck longevity is assured through the use of pressure-treated lumber is highly resistant to decay caused by both insect infestation and moisture.

● The handsome, functional awning installed

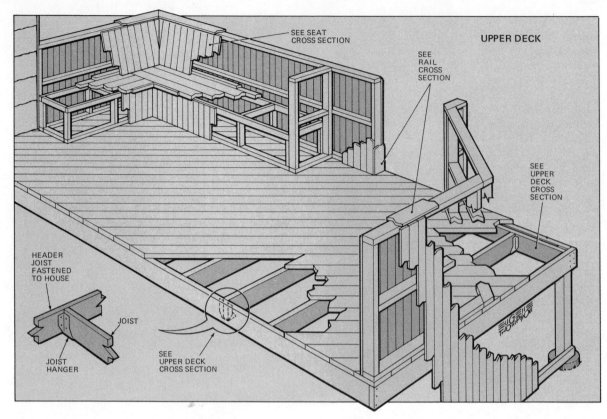

SEE SEAT CROSS SECTION

SEE RAIL CROSS SECTION

UPPER DECK

SEE UPPER DECK CROSS SECTION

HEADER JOIST FASTENED TO HOUSE

JOIST

JOIST HANGER

SEE UPPER DECK CROSS SECTION

over the upper level means that you will never have to cancel a cookout because of the weather. If rain threatens, the party can be moved to a table set up beneath the awning.

Where to start

Planning for the deck started with the family room at the rear of the house. The first floor elevation is roughly 36 in. above grade. This means that when the lower level is set on 2 x 6 joists, the upper level will be about 30 in. above. That height—which is the exact architectural standard for a dining table—inspired the built-in dining table here.

The upper deck was laid out to provide the all-weather aspect and a place was set aside for the built-in gas barbecue. The barbecue is located near the sliding doors, yet out of the flow of traffic across the upper level. Steps lead to the lower level, which boasts a deck with 2 x 6 boards laid diagonally over 2 x 6 joists.

Lay out your deck using mason's line and

LOWER-LEVEL JOISTS are fastened with two 16d galvanized common nails spiked through header joists. Use slate or pressure-treated wood as shims.

SOIL beneath the deck is covered with 6-mil polyethylene (or 30-lb. felt) to keep grass from growing through deck. Joists are spaced 16 in. on center.

THE 2 x 6 DECKING is installed with waste overhanging header. When all is down, a chalkline is snapped; decking is trimmed neatly with a portable saw.

stakes. You will need concrete piers to support posts for the upper level and these should be spaced no more than 8 ft. apart. You can use the anchor-bolt method, which requires boring a centered hole in the lower end of each post to accept the bolt. Or, install the posts into the holes, use diagonal bracing and stakes to hold them plumb, and pour a concrete collar around them. Both methods are good, but the latter is just a bit faster. If you are using pressure-treated lumber, the posts can rest in the ground without fear of rot.

Metal fasteners, which are available at all well-stocked lumberyards and home centers, speed up the framing chore considerably. The easiest way to frame the upper deck is thus:

1 Lay out for the header joist along the house wall. Do it so the finished decking will be 2 or 3 in. below the sill of the doorway to the house. Double-check your calculations. Snap a level chalkline along the house. Strip away siding or shingles so that the header can be installed flush against the sheathing. Re-snap the chalkline.

2 Run a bead of high-quality caulk along the chalkline and, with a helper, install the header

joist by nailing with 20d nails into the wall studs. Before nailing, make certain there is no chance of hitting any in-the-wall water or electric lines. Or, use lagscrews into the studs.

3 Install the *inside header joist only* at the outboard end by toenailing into the posts.

4 Next, lay out for and fasten the joist-hanger hardware, one on each end for each joist.

5 Measure, cut and install joists one at a time. Since there is just one header joist at the outboard end at this time, you can obtain great rigidity by spiking a couple of 16d common nails through it into each joist end.

6 When all joists are fastened, add the second 2 x 6 at the outboard end. Use plenty of 12d nails, driven at an angle, from both sides of the doubled-up beam.

7 Finish by installing the decking as shown. Use two 10d galvanized common nails in each board over each joist. Set all nailheads slightly below the surface using a large punch or heavy nailset.

8 When all decking is down, the overhanging waste can be cut off. To do it, partially drive nails above the outside edges of end joists and the

PLANTER AND utility table is framed with minimal number of 2 x 4s. One-inch siding, which follows, adds rigidity.

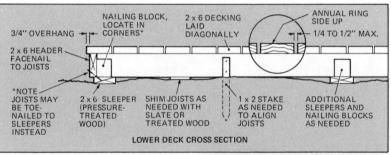
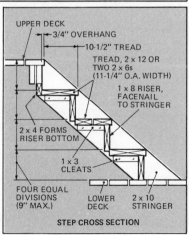

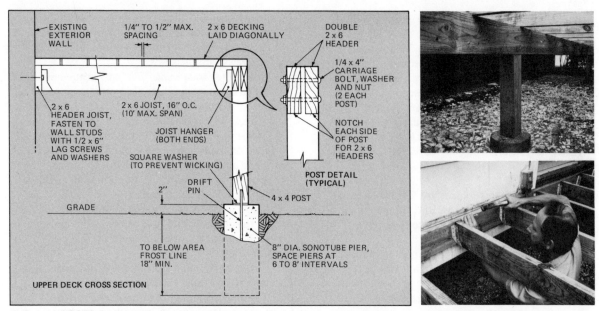

EXISTING EXTERIOR WALL

1/4" TO 1/2" MAX. SPACING

2 x 6 DECKING LAID DIAGONALLY

DOUBLE 2 x 6 HEADER

1/4 x 4" CARRIAGE BOLT, WASHER AND NUT (2 EACH POST)

2 x 6 HEADER JOIST, FASTEN TO WALL STUDS WITH 1/2 x 6" LAG SCREWS AND WASHERS

2 x 6 JOIST, 16" O.C. (10' MAX. SPAN)

JOIST HANGER (BOTH ENDS)

SQUARE WASHER (TO PREVENT WICKING)

DRIFT PIN

NOTCH EACH SIDE OF POST FOR 2 x 6 HEADERS

POST DETAIL (TYPICAL)

2"

4 x 4 POST

GRADE

TO BELOW AREA FROST LINE 18" MIN.

8" DIA. SONOTUBE PIER, SPACE PIERS AT 6 TO 8' INTERVALS

UPPER DECK CROSS SECTION

THE 4 x 4 POSTS for the upper level (upper right) are set over drift pins embedded in concrete piers (see drawing, above). Doubled-up 2 x 6s serve as the header joist on the outboard end. The header joist along the wall of the house (lower right) is nailed to the wall studs. The joists are installed using metal joist hangers.

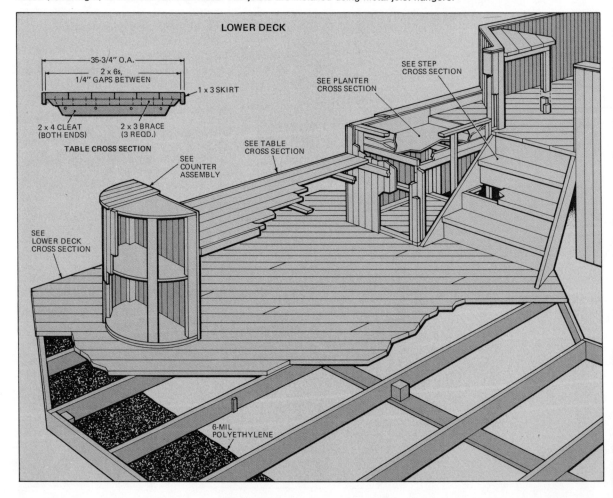

LOWER DECK

35-3/4" O.A.

2 x 6s, 1/4" GAPS BETWEEN

1 x 3 SKIRT

2 x 4 CLEAT (BOTH ENDS)

2 x 3 BRACE (3 REQD.)

TABLE CROSS SECTION

SEE STEP CROSS SECTION

SEE PLANTER CROSS SECTION

SEE COUNTER ASSEMBLY

SEE TABLE CROSS SECTION

SEE LOWER DECK CROSS SECTION

6-MIL POLYETHYLENE

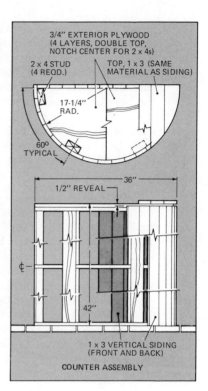

HALF-ROUND COUNTER is made with exterior plywood top and bottom and 2 x 4 studs. If desired, edges of 1 x 3 siding can be beveled for neat joints.

CLEAT SUPPORTING tabletop is fastened to counter to put dining table at 30-in. height. Use 1 x 3 boards for the tabletop, leaving a slight gap between boards.

Around image 3:
3/4" EXTERIOR PLYWOOD (4 LAYERS, DOUBLE TOP, NOTCH CENTER FOR 2 x 4s)
2 x 4 STUD (4 REQD.)
TOP, 1 x 3 (SAME MATERIAL AS SIDING)
17-1/4" RAD.
60° TYPICAL
36"
1/2" REVEAL
42"
1 x 3 VERTICAL SIDING (FRONT AND BACK)
COUNTER ASSEMBLY

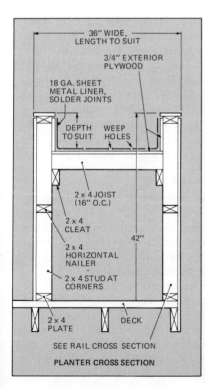

PLANTER CROSS SECTION
36" WIDE, LENGTH TO SUIT
3/4" EXTERIOR PLYWOOD
18 GA. SHEET METAL LINER, SOLDER JOINTS
DEPTH TO SUIT
WEEP HOLES
2 x 4 JOIST (16" O.C.)
2 x 4 CLEAT
2 x 4 HORIZONTAL NAILER
2 x 4 STUD AT CORNERS
42"
2 x 4 PLATE
DECK
SEE RAIL CROSS SECTION

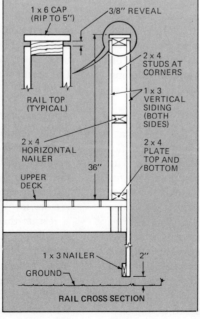

RAIL CROSS SECTION
1 x 6 CAP (RIP TO 5")
3/8" REVEAL
RAIL TOP (TYPICAL)
2 x 4 STUDS AT CORNERS
1 x 3 VERTICAL SIDING (BOTH SIDES)
2 x 4 HORIZONTAL NAILER
2 x 4 PLATE TOP AND BOTTOM
36"
UPPER DECK
1 x 3 NAILER
2"
GROUND

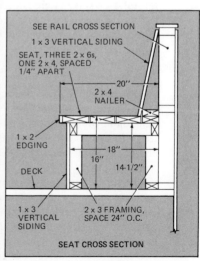

SEAT CROSS SECTION
SEE RAIL CROSS SECTION
1 x 3 VERTICAL SIDING
SEAT, THREE 2 x 6s, ONE 2 x 4, SPACED 1/4" APART
20"
2 x 4 NAILER
1 x 2 EDGING
18"
16"
14-1/2"
DECK
1 x 3 VERTICAL SIDING
2 x 3 FRAMING, SPACE 24" O.C.

header joist and snap a chalkline between nails. Make the cutoff using a combination blade in your circular saw with its blade set to just cut through the 1½-in.-thick decking. Cut on the outside of the waste line. If you make a wavy cut, you can true it up using a very coarse-grit paper (about 50-grit) in your belt sander. Don't start work on the upper-deck built-ins until after the lower deck has been completed. The stairs should be built only after both levels are finished.

The lower deck

There is nothing fancy or exotic about the way the lower deck is constructed. In fact, the simplest technique was used here because of the type of lumber.

With the deck's perimeter laid out, and corners checked for square, roll out either 6-mil polyethylene or 30-lb. felt. Either of these will keep grass from growing through the decking joints. Lay out the joists close to where they will be permanently installed. It will pay you to have a couple of long lengths of 1 x 3 furring on hand; these can be tacked across the top edges of the joists to keep them more or less in position, and on edge, while you get them all in place.

Once you have decided upon the elevation for the lower level, high ground spots will have to be excavated, if necessary, to bring a joist to the line. Conversely, a joist over a depression must be raised using either slate or pressure-treated wood scraps as shims.

You should also add stakes alongside joists at intervals to minimize deflection (bounce, as someone walks across the deck). The stakes are simply pointed 1 x 3s driven 18 to 24 in. into the ground and then nailed to joist sides. For rigidity, several 4 x 4 stakes were added at the corners on the deck shown. Once the diagonal 2 x 6 decking is installed, the lower level will have excellent stability.

The built-ins

As mentioned earlier, the dining table is at the same elevation as the upper deck, 30 in. The half-round counter at one end of the table is fitted with a cleat for the tabletop, and the other end of the top is secured to the upper deck, also with a cleat.

The top is constructed using 2 x 3s which, in turn, are skinned with 1 x 3 boards. The latter are installed with a slight gap between edges so food particles will drop through, rather than being caught between. The gap also makes it possible to clean the table using your garden hose.

The stairs between levels are easy to construct. They are built in conventional basement-stair fashion using 2 x 10 stringers and 2 x 12s for treads. Though the space between treads could be left open for an airy look, we installed risers on this prototype to hide the open space beneath the upper deck. The carriages (stringers) are not notched (cut out) to receive the risers and treads; instead, these are fastened to cleats securely nailed to the stringers. If you opt for notched stringers, you should use 2 x 12 stock for the stringers because there should be at least 3½ in. of solid timber beneath notches.

The stair assembly is fastened to the joist header at top by driving 16d nails through the stringers. The bottom of the stair carriage rests upon the lower level and is fastened to the latter with nails.

Calculating riser height

There is a definite relation between the width of a tread and the height of a riser. If the combination of run and rise is too great, there will be too much strain on the leg muscles and heart of the user. Too small a combination and the user will probably kick the riser on every step. (In the trades, this is often called a tripper.)

A good rule of thumb for laying out stairs is: the tread width multiplied by the riser height in inches should equal somewhere between 72 and 75 in. If your ratio is anywhere near that, you will have a comfortable-to-use stairway. (Another rule is that the tread width plus twice the riser height should be about 25 inches.) To lay out your stairs, simply divide the elevation to be negotiated by 7½ (the optimum riser height) to obtain the number of risers. If the elevation from lower deck to upper is about 30 in., as ours was, this means that four risers are needed (30 ÷ 7½ = 4). With 7½ in. risers, a 10-in. tread is desirable.

Professionals can help

The seating arrangement is obtained using straightforward, conventional framing. Once the seating is installed, the awning can go up. Since fabricating and installing an awning is a job best left to a professional, check the classified directory for the nearest awning dealer.

Rather than use a portable rollabout grill, we installed a fixed gas version. Since the pipe hookup should conform with local codes, it is best to have this connection made by your plumber. The bill will be lower if you have the plumber do the roughing-in when the deck is just framed out, before the decking goes down.

Perpetual desk calendar

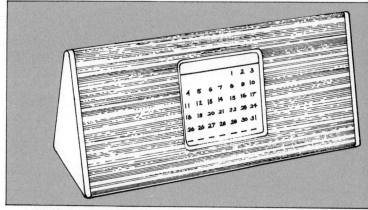

THE DESK calendar never needs replacing. Cut face from bottom of this page.

■ The dating system of this calendar is designed so it can be used forever. The calendar front is ⅛-in. lauan plywood surfaced with zebra-wood veneer, while the ends are solid cherry.

You can make the front and the number slider of any plywood or hardwood to match your decor. You'll need about one sq. ft. of this wood. Make the ends of hardwood (½ x 2½ x 7-in. piece) and the other parts of any solid wood.

Begin by carefully cutting the calendar from this page. Cut the front (A) and rough cut the window opening slightly undersize with a jigsaw or sabre saw. Use a jig to cut a bevel edge, front to back, on the window. First, center A in the jig, using the marked guidelines, and tack its corners with brads. Use a 45° bevel router bit with bearing guide. Adjust the bit for a ³⁄₁₆-in. depth of cut. Insert the router bit into the opening and allow the pilot to follow the opening in

the jig. Test on scrap wood first. After making the cut, remove the piece and sand the edges.

Next, cut stock to a ⁵⁄₃₂-in. thickness for the upper (C), lower (D) and end (E) spacers. Use rubber cement on both surfaces to mount the narrow paper strip (with the days of the week) on C. Cover the paper with clear adhesive film. Use white glue to secure C, so the print is properly aligned at the top of the window.

Cut the slider (B). Then cement the numeral sheet to B and cover with clear adhesive. Position the slider; then glue in the lower spacer (D), so slider can move freely.

Glue in the end spacers (E). To position them, place B behind the window, with No. 1 at the left edge of the window. This is the slider's left limit of travel. Repeat with No. 1 at the right-hand window edge.

AN INNER jig guides the router bit when you bevel cut around the window in piece A.

THE FACE can be cut as shown below or duplicated on a copying machine. Separate upper and lower sections with a single, straight cut.

Cut along dotted lines

						SUN	MON	TUE	WED	THU	FRI	SAT
						1	2	3	4	5	6	7
2	3	4	5	6	7	8	9	10	11	12	13	14
9	10	11	12	13	14	15	16	17	18	19	20	21
16	17	18	19	20	21	22	23	24	25	26	27	28
23	24	25	26	27	28	29	30	31	—	—	—	—
30	31	—	—	—	—	—	—	—	—	—	—	—

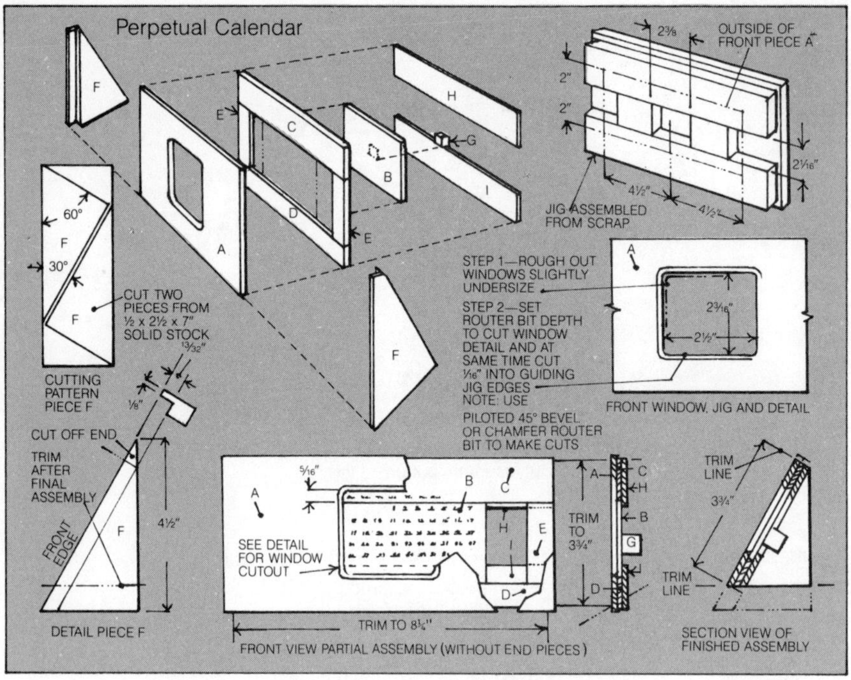
Perpetual Calendar
F
H
E
C
G
B
I
D
E
A
2⅜
OUTSIDE OF FRONT PIECE A
2"
2"
2⅛"
4½"
4½"
JIG ASSEMBLED FROM SCRAP
60°
30°
F
F
CUT TWO PIECES FROM ½ x 2½ x 7" SOLID STOCK
CUTTING PATTERN PIECE F
13/32"
1/8"
STEP 1—ROUGH OUT WINDOWS SLIGHTLY UNDERSIZE
STEP 2—SET ROUTER BIT DEPTH TO CUT WINDOW DETAIL AND AT SAME TIME CUT 1/16" INTO GUIDING JIG EDGES
NOTE: USE PILOTED 45° BEVEL OR CHAMFER ROUTER BIT TO MAKE CUTS
2 3/16"
2½"
FRONT WINDOW, JIG AND DETAIL
CUT OFF END
TRIM AFTER FINAL ASSEMBLY
FRONT EDGE
4½"
DETAIL PIECE F
5/16"
SEE DETAIL FOR WINDOW CUTOUT
TRIM TO 3¾"
TRIM TO 8⅛"
FRONT VIEW PARTIAL ASSEMBLY (WITHOUT END PIECES)
TRIM LINE
3¾"
TRIM LINE
SECTION VIEW OF FINISHED ASSEMBLY

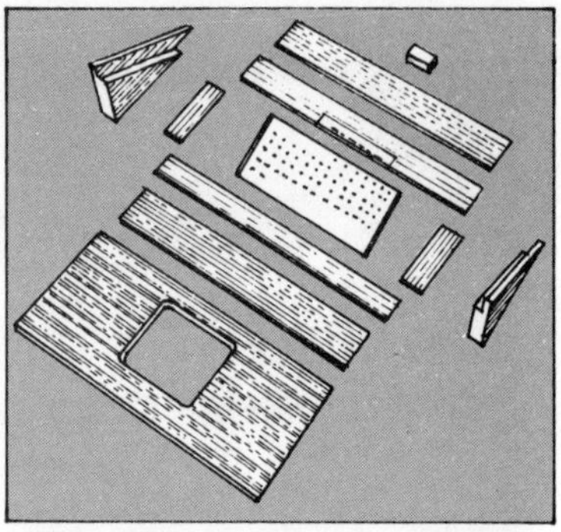

PARTS ARE cut and ready for assembly. Attach the days and numbers with rubber cement, cover with clear film.

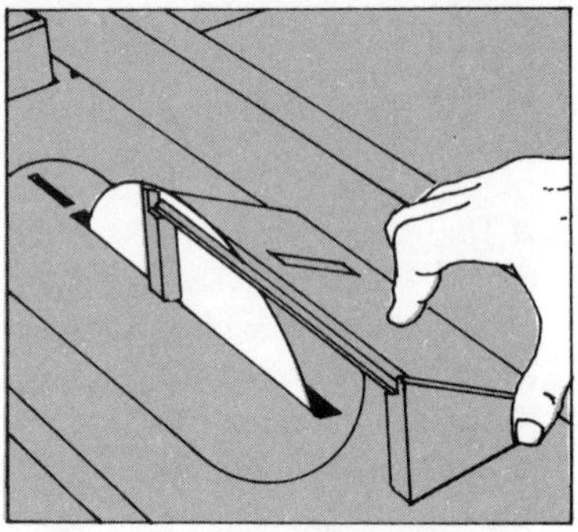

AFTER THE GLUE at side joints dries, place the stand face up, with top against the rip fence; trim bottom edge.

Cut the remaining parts. Clamp back strips (H and I) on the assembly for a trial front-to-back fit of the slider. If B fits too loosely, sand the back of the spacer strips. If it is too tight, sand its back. Glue G, H and I in place.

Trim the ends of the assembled front to size and attach end blocks (F) with glue. After the glue has dried, trim the bottom of edge A.

The stand is ready for final sanding and finishing. Oil the wood sparingly, then wax it. Varnish is not recommended as it may hinder the action of the slider.

Now the calendar is ready to use. For a given month, just move the slider until the number 1 is under the proper day of the week.

MATERIALS LIST—DESK CALENDAR

Key	No.	Size and description (use)
A	1	1/8 x 4 x 9" plywood or hardwood (front)
B	1	1/8 x 2 1/8 x 5 1/4" plywood or hardwood (slider)
C	1	5/32 x 1 1/8 x 9" solid wood (upper spacer)
D	1	5/32 x 5/8 x 9" solid wood (lower spacer)
E	2	5/32 x 3/4 x 2 1/8" solid wood (end spacer)
F	2	1/2 x 2 1/2 x 7" solid wood makes both pieces (end blocks)
G	1	1/2 x 1/2 x 1/2" solid wood (knob)
H	1	1/8 x 1 1/4 x 9" solid wood (top runner)
I	1	1/8 x 1 1/8 x 9" solid wood (bottom runner)

Misc.: Brads, white glue; sandpaper; clear film, such as Contact; rubber cement; Danish oil and wax or other finish.

THIS AREA TO BE CLIPPED OUT
SEE PREVIOUS PAGE

Stamp and pencil set

■ YOU'LL ALWAYS KNOW where to look for postage stamps when you have this novel dispenser on your desk. That goes for pens and pencils, too. It will hold two rolls of 100 stamps each, which are pulled out through slots in the side.

Wells for the stamps are bored in opposite sides of a hardwood cube (such as cherry or walnut) ½ in. up from the bottom and ½ in. in from the side. Entering kerfs are made through the side of the block with a thin-blade saw. Fancy metal buttons provide covers for the stamp wells and are held in place by small magnets that contact the heads of wood screws. The magnets are cemented to the backs of the buttons, and the screws around which the stamp rolls revolve are turned in far enough to bring the buttons flush.

Holes for pens and pencils are drilled down into the end grain of the block for a depth of 1½ in. and countersunk slightly. Complete by sanding the wood flawlessly, particularly the top of the block, and breaking the sharp corners. If the wood is open grain, you should apply a paste wood filler after staining, rubbing it off across grain. Finish by applying three coats of self-rubbing polyurethane varnish. When dry, glue a piece of green felt to the bottom of the block.

POSTAGE-STAMP SLOTS in the side of the block are cut through into the stamp wells with a thin-blade keyhole saw.

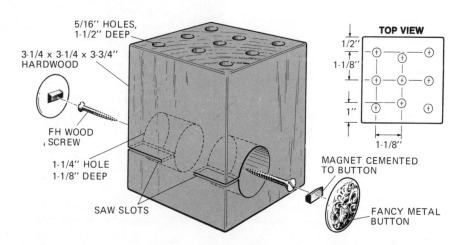

5/16" HOLES, 1-1/2" DEEP

3-1/4 x 3-1/4 x 3-3/4" HARDWOOD

FH WOOD SCREW

1-1/4" HOLE 1-1/8" DEEP

SAW SLOTS

MAGNET CEMENTED TO BUTTON

FANCY METAL BUTTON

TOP VIEW

1/2"

1-1/8"

1"

1-1/8"

Calculator stand

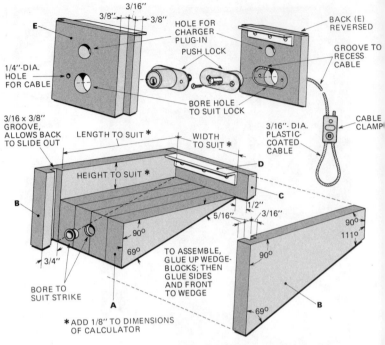

WHEN STAND is unlocked, back of calculator can be raised for removal. Suit dimensions to your calculator.

■ POCKET CALCULATORS have a tendency to "grow legs and walk off" without a stand such as this one.

Begin by tracing the side (profile) of your calculator. Add ⅛ in. to the overall length and height. Next, draw in the area for the bottom wedges and back and front panels. Use this diagram as a pattern to cut out sides B and wedges A.

Following the drawing, cut the wedge and side sections, glue together, then glue on the front. Bore a hole for the lock in the back. Then mortise the lock flush. Drill a hole through back of lock faceplate for cable and cut a small groove under the faceplate to hold it.

Bore holes in the back large enough for the lock and charger plug. Cut and drill two pieces of aluminum angle. Each should be attached flush with the top of the case.

STAND MAKES calculator easier to read. Cable prevents the

MATERIALS LIST—STAND

Key	No.	Size and description (use)
A	4 or 5	¾" pine; short side of wedge is 1¾" long; other dimensions to suit (base)
B	2	½" hardwood to suit (side)
C	1	½" hardwood to suit (front)
D	2	½ x ½" aluminum angle to suit (retainers)
E	1	¾" hardwood to suit
Misc.:		Push lock, cable clamp, ³⁄₁₆"-dia. plastic-coated cable x length to suit

Gadgets to hold everything

■ **THIS NOVEL DRILL** holder is fancy enough to use most anywhere to corral many things other than just drills. If you are familiar with the egg-shaped plastic containers in which panty hose are packaged, you'll be quick to see that the ready-made dome shapes do the holding. As the two photos show, you first drill a circle of holes in the top of each half shell, using each bit to drill its own hole, and drilling from the inside out. Then you cut a 2-in Styrofoam ball in half, glue the pieces inside the half shells and finally cement the shells to a suitable wood base. Each drill bit is poked into the Styrofoam through a hole in the top of the shell.

Equally as eye-catching and handy as a desk accessory is the pen and pencil holder shown at the right. The twin cylinders are turned and grooved two at a time on a lathe from aluminum to represent revolver chambers, then bored from the top to accept pencils and ballpoint pens.

PAD THE VISE JAWS with leather when drilling the holes. Start with a small bit, then switch to a larger one.

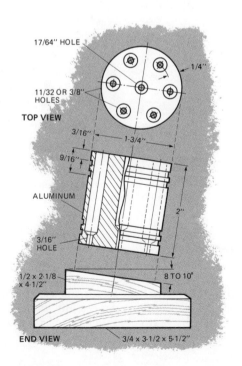

17/64" HOLE

1/4"

11/32 OR 3/8" HOLES

TOP VIEW

3/16"

1-3/4"

9/16"

ALUMINUM

2"

3/16" HOLE

1/2 x 2-1/8 x 4-1/2"

8 TO 10°

END VIEW

3/4 x 3-1/2 x 5-1/2"

LINE THE SHELL with masking tape to keep the drill bit from wandering. Drill the holes from the inside.

CUT THE STYROFOAM balls in half and glue inside the shells. Drills are poked into the foam from the top.

Start with a $^3/_{16}$-in. drill bit to drill the seven holes from top to bottom, then redrill to final size with a larger bit for a depth of 1⅝ in. Drill a couple of holes at a time, take a coffee break to allow the metal to cool to avoid overheating, then continue. One cylinder should be drilled to hold slender pens, the other to take fatter ones.

After polishing with fine abrasive cloth and chamfering the holes a wee bit to remove burrs, attach each cylinder to a two-piece prefinished walnut base with a single wood screw down through the center hole.

By cutting the wood base longer, you can make the holder even more useful with a well between the cylinders to hold paper clips, stamps, or a rack to hold letters.

Letter racks to organize your mail

COLONIAL

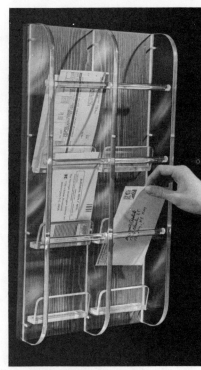

CONTEMPORARY

■ IF YOUR INCOMING mail gets tossed on the nearest counter or table when you walk in the door, build one of our handsome letter organizers. It will put an end to the clutter, confusion and annoyance of mislaid letters. The contemporary-styled organizer is made with clear-acrylic sheet dividers and retainers and a pine backboard. The colonial-styled unit is made entirely of clear pine.

Making the colonial organizer

Start by cutting board A from a piece of 1x12 clear pine and all other parts from ½-in. stock. Use a jig, coping or bandsaw with narrow blade to make the scroll cut at top. The shaped sides (D) can be ganged together and cut and sanded in a single operation. The same goes for the compartment fronts (B).

All edges are rounded with a rounding-over router bit. The small pieces are best handled on a router accessory table, which lets the router function as a shaper. Parts are simply passed against the cutter. Lacking the table, clamp workpieces to your workbench and use the router in the usual manner.

Assembling compartment members to center board (E) is tricky because nails can't be driven through from both sides. However, protruding nails can be used to assure alignment for gluing. Clip heads from nails and bore pilot holes for

nails on inner edges (those that abut E) of six compartment fronts (B). Push nails into holes with points protruding about ¼ in. Tack-nail side pieces (D) to the compartment sections. Then press parts together against center dividing strip (E). Do this step on a flat surface.

Since the shape of this rack is too confining to permit successful application of stain, it is important to stain *before* assembly. While the unit is temporarily assembled with nails, mark outlines of all butt joints with a pencil. Then disassemble. Apply masking tape to all outlined surfaces. This keeps stain from areas to be glued.

After staining all parts except the outsides of the side members (D), remove the tape and reassemble the rack with glue. Outsides are stained later because they must be sanded flush with the back after gluing. Apply a varnish spray coat to completed assembly.

The contemporary organizer

Start by cutting the verticals (A,B) using a fine-tooth plywood blade (see drawing). Gang the three pieces together with masking tape and cut the round corners at the same time using a bandsaw, if available, or cut the corners individually with a sabre or coping saw. Be *certain* to leave the protective masking paper intact during all machining and finishing operations.

Use a scraper or sharp chisel with a pulling

SCROLL patterns on colonial-style organizer can be cut with jigsaw, bandsaw with narrow blade, or coping saw.

TO SAVE time, side members (D) are taped together before cutting scroll. Use a sharp blade and slow feed.

SAND convex curves with sander/grinder. Use drum sander, drill, or drill press to smooth concave curves.

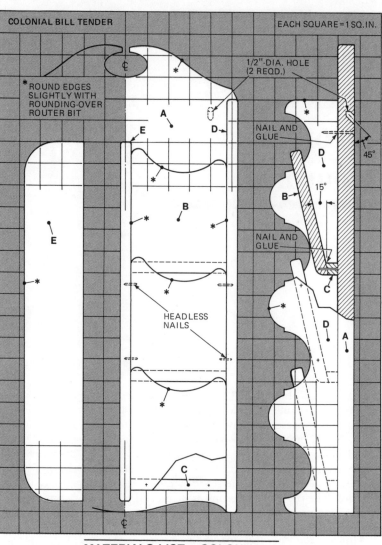

COLONIAL BILL TENDER   EACH SQUARE = 1 SQ. IN.

*ROUND EDGES SLIGHTLY WITH ROUNDING-OVER ROUTER BIT

1/2"-DIA. HOLE (2 REQD.)

NAIL AND GLUE

45°

15°

NAIL AND GLUE

HEADLESS NAILS

MATERIALS LIST—COLONIAL ORGANIZER

Key	Pcs.	Size and description
A	1	¾ × 10½" clear pine
B	6	½ × 4½ × 5¾" clear pine
C	6	½ × ⅝ × 4½" clear pine
D	2	½ × 3¼ × 19" clear pine
E	1	½ × 2¾ × 16½" clear pine

Misc: White glue, nails to suit.

ROUTER table simplifies rounding-over the edges; use a piloted bit to make a pass on both sides of the work.

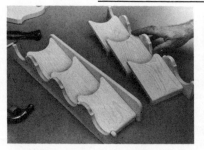

BEFORE gluing, use protruding-nail trick to align halves of organizer with central divider (see text).

TRACE JOINT locations and mask them with tape. Apply stain to pieces. When they are dry, reassemble with glue.

stroke to smooth out all saw marks. Follow up by sanding all edges with silicon carbide paper, working up from 220 to 600 grit.

Next, bore all holes and tap where necessary. Be particularly careful when drilling blind holes in (B) pieces. Since masking paper conceals view, make test borings in scrap to get it right. Cut shelf pieces with appropriate bevels. Then cement front pieces (D) to bases (E) with solvent cement.

The solvent works by capillary action, which requires that surfaces to be joined be in close contact. To obtain the necessary smooth, flat surface on the beveled edges of the fronts, do this: After smoothing edges with a chisel or scraper,

lay a sheet of abrasive paper face up on a flat surface. Stroke workpiece firmly back and forth, making sure not to rock it. Work with progressively finer grits of silicon carbide paper. After sanding the beveled edges of the fronts, do the same to the beveled edges of base pieces. Sand remainder after cementing.

Remove the protective masking paper before cementing. Use masking tape to hold parts together. A fine-nozzle, squeeze-bottle cement applicator, available where you buy the acrylic, is used to apply cement. Lay assemblies down so the joint is horizontal. Apply a thin line of cement on joint line. If pieces are in good contact,

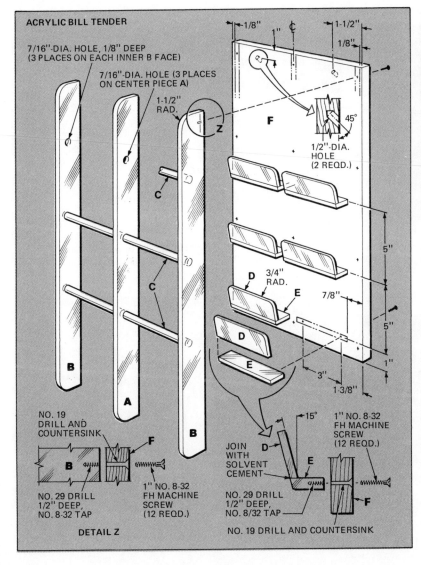

TO CUT parts from acrylic sheet, use a fine-tooth veneer blade elevated about ⅛-in. above the workpiece.

USE TAP to cut threads in plastic. Stop twisting when tap meets resistance; use soap for lubrication.

cement will be sucked in and quickly weld the joint. Don't touch parts for five minutes.

Sand all the flat edges of the shelves and slightly round the front bottom corners. Also cut and sand the rounds on the upper corners.

All edges which do not contact wood backboard are polished to a high gloss by buffing with polishing compound. Use a buffing wheel, or a soft cloth shoeshine fashion.

If the screws meet resistance during assembly, rub a bit of soap on them. Attach two of the uprights; then insert the ⅜-in. rods before adding the third upright. The backboard is given a finish of walnut stain and satin topcoat varnish. (Do this before attaching the acrylic parts. Clear acrylic sheets and rods are available at some home centers and at plastics supply houses. Look in Yellow Pages under "Plastics—Sheets & Rods."

MATERIALS LIST—MODERN LOCATER

Key	Pcs.	Size and description
A	1	⅜ × 3 × 21" clear acrylic plastic
B	2	⅜ × 3 × 21" clear acrylic plastic
C	3	⅜"-dia. x 9¾" clear acrylic plastic
D	6	¼ × 1½ × 4" clear acrylic plastic
E	6	⅜ × 1⅛ × 4" clear acrylic plastic
F	1	¾ × 10½ × 21" clear pine

Misc: Solvent cement, screws to suit.

USE A cabinet scraper or sharp chisel to remove saw ripples. Upright dividers are ganged to save time.

FOR CLEAN holes, run drill press at high speed. Set depth so bit stops 1/16 in. from bottom of B pieces.

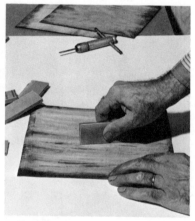

RUB EDGES of parts to be glued against abrasive sheet to obtain a perfect flat.

REMOVE protective masking paper, tape parts together and apply solvent—with the joint line horizontal.

AFTER SANDING edges with 600-grit paper, polish on buffing wheel charged with auto-polishing compound.

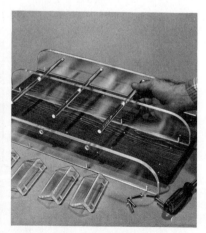

INSERT retaining rods (C) before screwing on last divider. Pine backboard should be finished first.

Desk for home offices

■ REMEMBER the old rolltop desk—how you could pull down the front and walk away without disturbing your work? You can do practically the same with this modern version which has wraparound wings that close like the twin doors on a refrigerator.

Posing as a king-size chest when closed, the desk features a swing-out shelf that provides a regulation-height typing stand. Two paper-storage compartments in the wings are within easy reach of your chair. A shallow under-the-desk drawer keeps pens, pencils, clips and the like extra handy. Important papers can be stored safely and locked in a fireproof steel filing cabinet. There's a shelf for a wastebasket and drawers galore for storing countless supplies. A built-in fluorescent light is supplemented by a mini typing spotlight.

The unit is designed around a two-drawer metal file cabinet and built largely from ¾ in. plywood covered with handsome woodgrain plastic laminate.

File cabinets come in various sizes, but to obtain a regulation desk height of 30 in. and a standard typing shelf of 26 in., you must select a cabinet that measures 29¼ in. high. Width and depth are not so important; the cabinet shown measures 15 in. wide and 27¾ in. deep.

WHEN WINGS ARE SWUNG SHUT, office fits in a 29x43x48-in. chest. Swung open wide, wings provide spacious work center measuring 7½ ft.

WINGS WRAP AROUND FILE CABINET on one side (see left), desk on other. Swinging typing shelf parks under desk drawer when not in use.

The chest consists of three separate sections—a center section and two wings. The cutting schedule shows how the 16 basic parts can be economically laid out on two 4x8-ft. sheets of ¾-in. plywood. Although it costs a bit more than common fir plywood, cabinet-grade lumber-core plywood was used in the original. It is less susceptible to warping and has a smoother surface for painting.

Begin making the center section which includes parts E and F. Parts E are 14⅝ x 47⅝ in., part F is 14⅝ x 43 in. A ⅜ x ⅜-in. rabbet is cut along the rear edges of all three parts, and a ⅜ x ¾-in. rabbet is cut across each end of part F. Glue and nail part F to parts E, then enclose the back with a ⅜-in. plywood panel, 42¼ x 47⅝ in. Glue two 2 x 29¼-in. strips of ⅛-in. tempered hardboard vertically to the inside of part E at points X, front and back. These will bring the file cabinet flush with the right-hand side of the desktop and provide clearance for the right-hand wing.

Make the desktop and drawer next. Remember that dimensions given accommodate a 15 x 28-in. file cabinet. Note that the top is ⅜ in. wider at the back than the front and that it's made double-thick except where it rests on top of the file cabinet. A ¾ x 1 x 14-in. cleat is screwed to the inside of part E (29¼ in. high) to support the desktop along the left-hand edge. Holes are made in the bottom of the cleat for attaching the desktop with 1¼-in. No. 8 fh screws. Screw holes are also made across the plywood back and in the top of the metal file cabinet, although the desktop is not permanently installed at this time.

Except for being right and left-handed, with the left wing having a shelf at the bottom, both wings are made alike. Parts A measure 14⅝ x 46⅝ in. and have a ½ x ¾-in. rabbet along the front edges to accept parts B, which measure 21³/₁₆ x 46⅝ in. The latter are glued and nailed in the rabbets with finish nails and checked for squareness. Parts C measure 14⅝ x 21⁷/₁₆ in. and are rabbeted (⅜ x ¾ in.) along two edges to fit over and flush with the top edges of parts A and B, then glued and nailed. Part D (the wing shelf) is secured with ¾-in.-square cleats glued and screwed to parts A and B. Screw holes for attaching shelf brace L are drilled through parts B and D for screws driven from the front and up from the bottom.

The actual length of part I is determined by the width of the file cabinet. In the original it measures 14 x 26⅜ in. and is anchored in place by a cleat at one end and the file cabinet at the other. Two holes are drilled through the side of the cabinet for screws from the inside.

The 14 x 21-in. swing-away typewriter shelf consists of parts H, J and K. Parts J and K are glued and screwed along adjacent edges of part H. A 10-in. length of piano hinge is used to hinge the assembled shelf to a ¾ x 2 x 10-in. wood block, which is later screwed and glued to the inside of part E, 26 in. up from the floor.

Now you are ready to cover the various parts and assemblies with plastic laminate. It takes

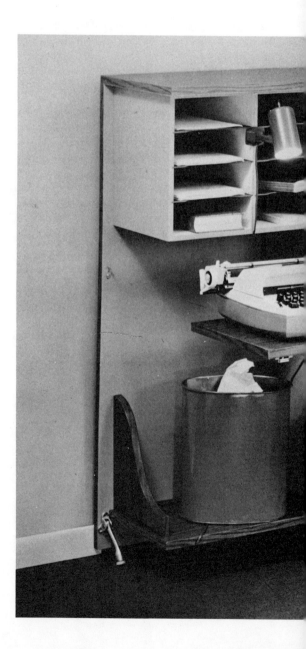

about two and a half 4x8-ft. sheets.

The most professional (and fastest) trimming job is done with a portable router, using special cutters, but it can be done with a special hand tool.

Only part L is covered with laminate on both sides, others just on the edge and one side. In each case, the edges are banded first. A good place to start is on parts D and L since these, particularly part L, must be screwed in place before part B can be covered on the outside. In the case of the wings, the extra width that the 1/16-in. laminate adds has been accounted for in the overall sizes given for parts B and C. Inside surfaces not covered with laminate were painted olive green, as was the file cabinet. Here it's wise to paint the back panel of the center section before assembling the desk.

When all parts are covered with laminate, you can start putting the desk together. First lay the

center section on its back and position the file cabinet against the ⅛-in. hardboard strips. Use two C-clamps to hold the cabinet in place and drill two screw holes through the sheet metal opposite each hardboard strip. Drill two more through the back of the file cabinet and the plywood back. Use ¾-in. No. 8 rh wood screws into the hardboard strips, and ¾-in. stovebolts through the plywood back.

Next install the desktop by turning screws up through the left-hand cleat, through holes in the top of the file cabinet and holes in the plywood back. Add the typewriter shelf by screwing the block to which it is hinged to part E at a point 26 in. up from the floor. The shelf should clear the desk drawer by ¼ in. Part I is added next and is held with screws inserted through its cleat, the side of the file cabinet and the plywood back.

Wings are hinged last with 46¼-in.-long piano hinges. It's best to hold the wings in their open position by clamping them temporarily to the sides of the center section. Hinges are surface-mounted.

The striker plate from a lockset is used to align the two wings with the top of the center section when they are swung shut. Two magnetic catches, screwed to the underside of the desktop at the front, are used to hold the doors shut. A third magnetic catch is used to hold the typewriter shelf closed, while an elbow catch is used to lock the shelf in open position. The plate for the magnetic catch on the typewriter shelf is fastened to the plywood back with a short stovebolt. A pivoted doorstop is used to keep the left-hand door "locked" to the floor when the typing shelf is being used.

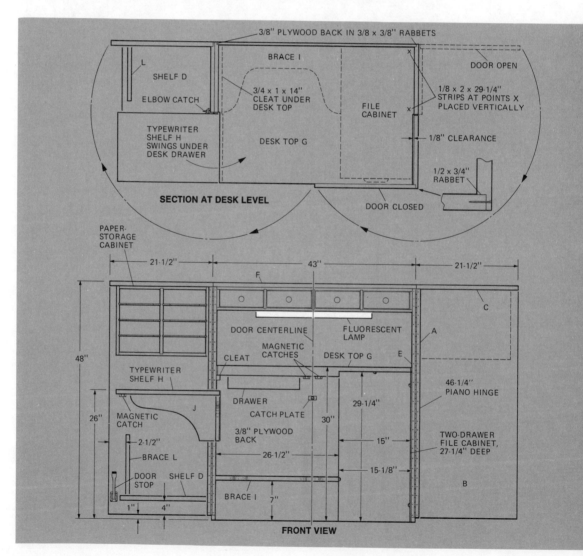

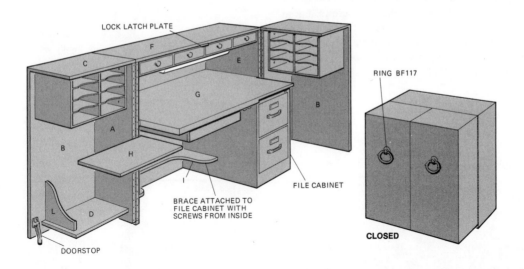

LOCK LATCH PLATE

C

F

E

B

G

A

B

H

I

L

D

DOORSTOP

BRACE ATTACHED TO
FILE CABINET WITH
SCREWS FROM INSIDE

FILE CABINET

RING BF117

CLOSED

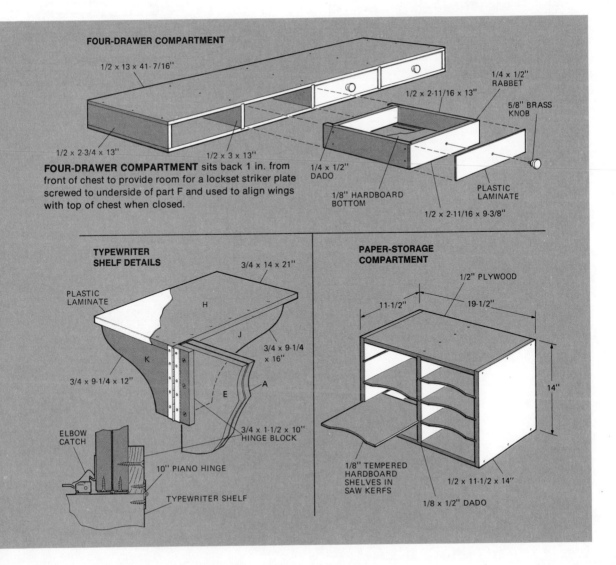

FOUR-DRAWER COMPARTMENT

1/2 x 13 x 41-7/16"

1/4 x 1/2"
RABBET

1/2 x 2-11/16 x 13"

5/8" BRASS
KNOB

1/2 x 2-3/4 x 13"

1/2 x 3 x 13"

1/4 x 1/2"
DADO

1/8" HARDBOARD
BOTTOM

PLASTIC
LAMINATE

1/2 x 2-11/16 x 9-3/8"

FOUR-DRAWER COMPARTMENT sits back 1 in. from
front of chest to provide room for a lockset striker plate
screwed to underside of part F and used to align wings
with top of chest when closed.

**TYPEWRITER
SHELF DETAILS**

3/4 x 14 x 21"

PLASTIC
LAMINATE

H

J

3/4 x 9-1/4
x 16"

K

3/4 x 9-1/4 x 12"

E

A

ELBOW
CATCH

3/4 x 1-1/2 x 10"
HINGE BLOCK

10" PIANO HINGE

TYPEWRITER SHELF

**PAPER-STORAGE
COMPARTMENT**

1/2" PLYWOOD

11-1/2"

19-1/2"

14"

1/8" TEMPERED
HARDBOARD
SHELVES IN
SAW KERFS

1/2 x 11-1/2 x 14"

1/8 x 1/2" DADO

Twin paper-storage bins, and the four-drawer compartment, are held in place by screws. Large decorative towel rings are used for elegant wing pulls, and a regular 24-in. undercabinet fluorescent fixture attaches to the underside of the drawer compartment.

CUTTING SCHEDULE

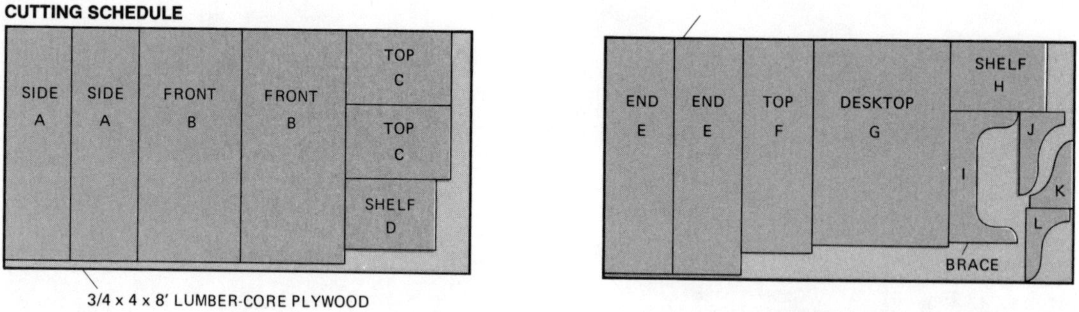
SIDE A
SIDE A
FRONT B
FRONT B
TOP C
TOP C
SHELF D
3/4 x 4 x 8' LUMBER-CORE PLYWOOD
END E
END E
TOP F
DESKTOP G
SHELF H
I
J
K
L
BRACE

ACTUAL CUTTING SIZES

(A) ¾ x 14⅝ x 46⅝ in.—Wing sides
(B) ¾ x 21 3/16 x 46⅝ in.—Wing fronts
(C) ¾ x 14⅝ x 21 7/16 in.—Wing tops
(D) ¾ x 12 x 18¼ in.—Wing shelf
(E) ¾ x 14⅝ x 47⅝ in. —Chest ends
(F) ¾ x 14⅝ x 43 in.—Chest top
(G) ¾ x 28 x 40⅛ in.—Desk top
(H) ¾ x 14 x 21 in.—Typewriter shelf
(I) ¾ x 14 x 26⅜ in.—Brace
(J) ¾ x 9¼ x 16 in.—Typewriter-shelf brace
(K) ¾ x 9¼ x 12 in.—Typewriter-shelf brace
(L) ¾ x 9¼ x 11 in.—Wing-shelf brace

UNDERSIDE OF DESKTOP

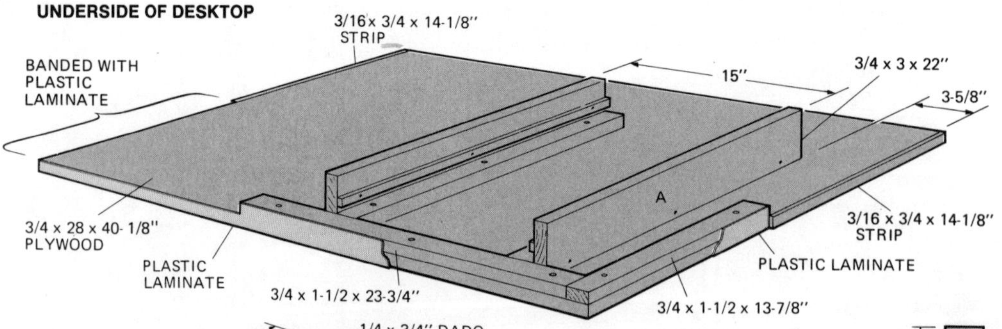
3/16 x 3/4 x 14-1/8" STRIP
BANDED WITH PLASTIC LAMINATE
15"
3/4 x 3 x 22"
3-5/8"
A
3/4 x 28 x 40-1/8" PLYWOOD
PLASTIC LAMINATE
3/4 x 1-1/2 x 23-3/4"
3/16 x 3/4 x 14-1/8" STRIP
PLASTIC LAMINATE
3/4 x 1-1/2 x 13-7/8"

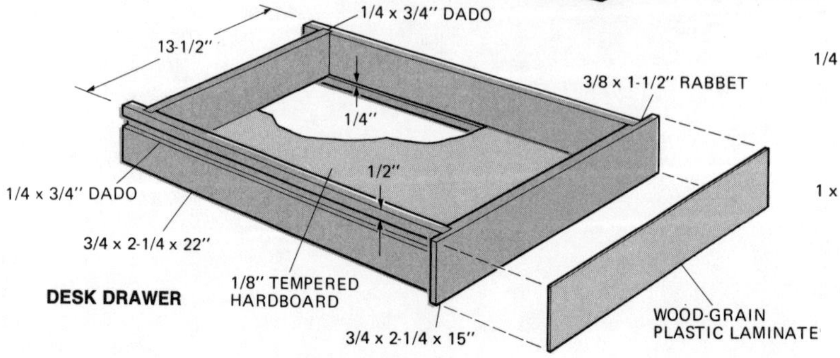
1/4 x 3/4" DADO
13-1/2"
3/8 x 1-1/2" RABBET
1/4"
1/2"
1/4 x 3/4" DADO
3/4 x 2-1/4 x 22"
1/8" TEMPERED HARDBOARD
3/4 x 2-1/4 x 15"
WOOD-GRAIN PLASTIC LAMINATE

DESK DRAWER

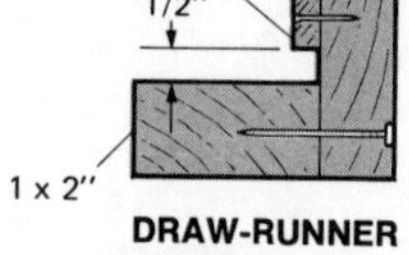
1"
1/4 x 11/16"
1/2"
A
1 x 2"

DRAW-RUNNER DETAIL

Colonial trestle desk

■ HERE'S AN EARLY AMERICAN reproduction that you and your family will treasure for years to come—a charming colonial trestle desk.

To copy this fine period piece, start with parts A and B, the desk's top and bottom. Cut six boards ¾ x 8 x 57½ in. Then glue, dowel and clamp them together edgewise to make two ¾ x 24 x 57½ in. panels. When the glue dries, trim the panels to a finished width of 23¼ in.

Desk ends. Cut four pieces 5½ x 24 in. from 1¼-in. stock and glue them together to make two 11x24-in. boards, using bar clamps and dowel pins. Next, glue and dowel ⅝ x 1¼-in. pieces

(end caps) to the ends of the glued-up end pieces to conceal the end grain. Now lay out the ends, following the shape and dimensions given. Cut to size and shape and round the four outer edges of each.

Assembly of top members. The narrow top shelf measures ¾ x 5¾ x 57½ in. After a thorough sanding, position the top, bottom and shelf members against the ends and mark. Allow a 4-in. space between the three to accommodate drawers. Position the top member ½ in. down from the top of the ends and ¾ in. from the rear to leave space for a ¾-in. backboard. Next, drill

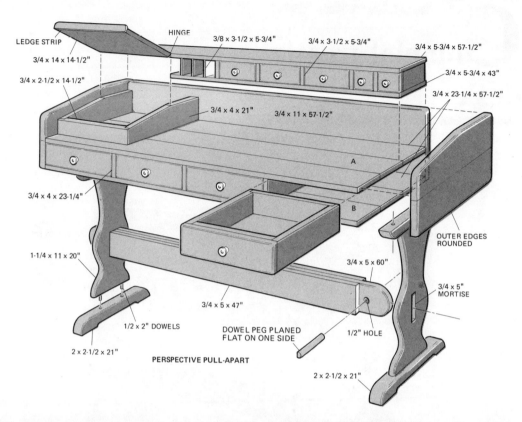

LEDGE STRIP

HINGE

3/8 x 3-1/2 x 5-3/4"

3/4 x 3-1/2 x 5-3/4"

3/4 x 5-3/4 x 57-1/2"

3/4 x 14 x 14-1/2"

3/4 x 5-3/4 x 43"

3/4 x 2-1/2 x 14-1/2"

3/4 x 23-1/4 x 57-1/2"

3/4 x 4 x 21"

3/4 x 11 x 57-1/2"

A

3/4 x 4 x 23-1/4"

B

OUTER EDGES ROUNDED

1-1/4 x 11 x 20"

3/4 x 5 x 60"

3/4 x 5" MORTISE

1/2 x 2" DOWELS

3/4 x 5 x 47"

DOWEL PEG PLANED FLAT ON ONE SIDE

1/2" HOLE

2 x 2-1/2 x 21"

PERSPECTIVE PULL-APART

2 x 2-1/2 x 21"

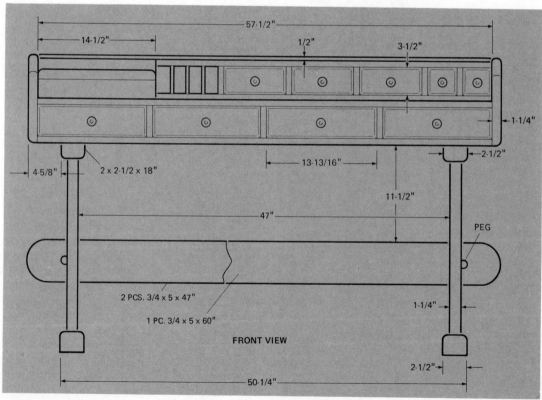

57-1/2"

14-1/2"

1/2"

3-1/2"

1-1/4"

13-13/16"

2-1/2"

4-5/8"

2 x 2-1/2 x 18"

11-1/2"

47"

PEG

2 PCS. 3/4 x 5 x 47"

1 PC. 3/4 x 5 x 60"

1-1/4"

FRONT VIEW

2-1/2"

50-1/4"

ACCESS TO slant-top storage compartment at left side of desk is by its hinged writing surface, which lifts.

and counterbore the ends for No. 10 x 1½-in. flathead (fh) screws, spacing them evenly for attaching the top, shelf and bottom members. Use glue, drive the screws, plug the counterbored holes and sand.

Hinged-lid compartment. Cut the front piece ¾ x 2½ x 14½ in. and the two side members ¾ x

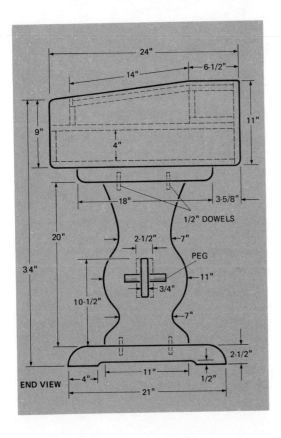

24"
14"
6-1/2"
9"
4"
11"
18"
3-5/8"
1/2" DOWELS
20"
2-1/2"
7"
PEG
34"
11"
3/4"
10-1/2"
7"
2-1/2"
END VIEW
4"
11"
1/2"
21"

4 x 21 in. Preassemble the compartment, then install the members with glue and screws. The grain of the hinged lid should run crosswise or the same direction as the desktop grain. Here ¾ x 1-in. strips are added to the end-grain edges. Overall size of the lid should measure 14 x 14½ in. including a ⅜ x 1-in. strip added to the front edge. Attach the compartment's lid with a 1¹¹/₁₆-in.-wide piano hinge.

Drawer and envelope compartments. Cut the drawer separators 4 in. wide and glue them in place between the top and bottom members and between top and shelf. Make sure the separators are installed squarely and parallel, using glue and brads. Separators for envelope pigeon holes should be cut from ⅜-in. stock.

Drawers are made following simple rabbet and butt-joint construction and fitted to slide freely in the opening. The sides and backs are of ⅜-in. stock, fronts are ¾ in. and all are grooved to accept ⅛-in. hardboard bottoms.

Desk back. Cut a ¾-in. board to size of 11 x 57½ in. for the back. Round the top edge and attach the board from the back and from the end with fh screws in counterbored holes. Plug the holes with screw buttons and sand flush.

Cut two pieces from 1¼-in. stock 12x20 in. for the legs. Lay out the pieces following dimensions, bandsaw them, cut the ¾ x 5-in. rail mortises and sand the edges. Next cut the 2 x 2½-in. head and foot pieces and dowel them to the top and bottom ends of the legs. Note that No. 10 x 1½-in. fh screws are used in countersunk holes in the top cross members to attach the legs to the upper assembly.

Glue together the three members that make up the 2¼-in.-thick rail (trestle), letting the center member project at each end to form a shouldered tenon. Drill ½-in. holes in the tenons for the cross pegs. The latter should be cut from scrap and shaped to rough form.

Finishing. The desk is now ready for its final sanding with No. 150 grit or finer sandpaper. After sanding it smooth, apply a dark stain that will enhance the grain structure in the pine. If you prefer varnish to lacquer because of its ability to resist water spots, use a satin finish. Spray on five coats, sand the desk lightly between coats with No. 280 sandpaper and clean the finish with a tack rag.

After the fifth coat, sand it ever so lightly with the 280-grit paper and then apply four coats of paste wax with a 000 steel wool pad. Finally, follow this with 10 more coats of paste wax, buffing these coats to a soft luster with a soft cloth.

CAMPAIGN DESK is patterned after the British military desk used by upper-echelon field officers.

Campaign desk

■ THE 19TH-CENTURY British officer's campaign desk is experiencing a revival. The originals had leather tops embellished in hand-tooled gold leaf, metal-bound corners and recessed drawer pulls. They rested on detachable trestles.

PM's version has retained these features, with minor exceptions. Naugahyde and gold leaf are substituted for real leather. An optional top treatment, also illustrated, uses leather-textured plastic laminate embellished with decals.

The desktop is made up in picture-frame form, with a deep rabbet on the inside to permit the "leather" surfaced insert panel to set in flush. This is a simplified and very practical method of inlaying the material. The advantage is that the

MATERIALS LIST—CAMPAIGN-STYLE DESK

Key	Pcs.	Size and description	Key	Pcs.	Size and description
A	1	½ X 20½ X 44½" fir plywood	J	2	½ x 5 x 12-5/16" poplar
B	2	13/16 x 2½ x 24" cherry	K	6	½ x 5 x 22" poplar
C	3	13/16 x 2½ x 48" cherry	L	2	13/16 x 5 x 12-5/16" cherry
D	1	13/16 x 5⅜ x 46⅞" cherry	M	2	¼ x 11¾ x 21¾" hardboard
E	2	13/16 x 5⅜ x 24"	N	1	½ x 5 x 20¼" poplar
		(less width of wood strips	O	1	13/16 x 5 x 20¼" cherry
		that conceal end grain) cherry	P	1	¼ x 19¾ x 21¾" hardboard
F	2	13/16 x 5⅜ x 23-7/16" cherry	Q	8	13/16 x 2 x 25" cherry
G	1	¾ x 22 x 46" fir plywood	R	8	13/16 x 2 x 20½" cherry
H	2	¾ x 1 x 24" cherry	S	4	13/16 x 2 x 20¼" cherry
I	2	¾ x 1 x 48" cherry	T	4	13/16 x 2¼ x 20½" cherry

Misc. ⅔ yard Naugahyde or laminated plastic

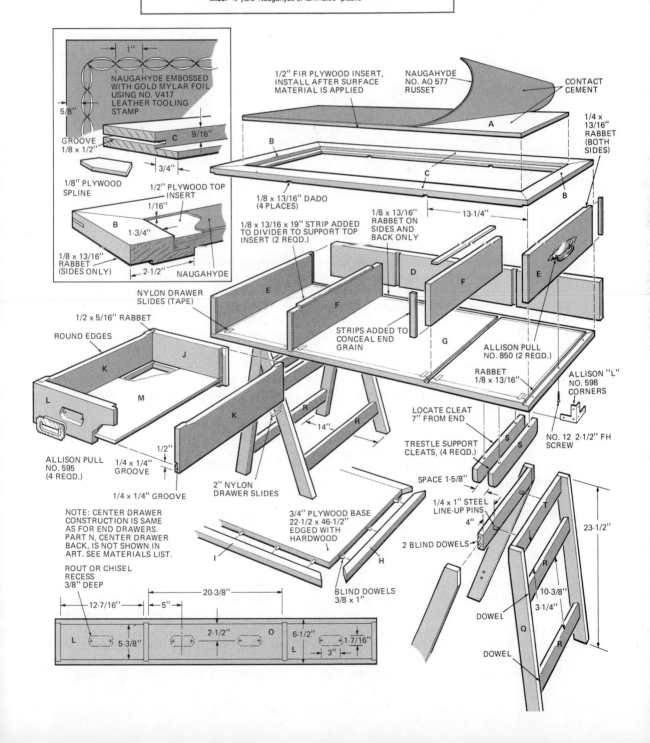

BUILDING THE DESK

1 MITER JIG slides in miter-gauge grooves, makes mitering frame easier.

2 USE fence-riding jig to cut grooves for splines at corners. See drawing.

3 USE hold-down block, auxiliary wood fence for inboard rabbets.

4 JOIN cross members, back to base with screws, glue. Add top, glue, clamp.

5 SIMPLE jig can be used for cutting angles needed on leg tops.

6 USE small nails, with heads removed, to mark dowel-hole centers.

Naugahyde, or plastic laminate, can easily be cemented and edge-trimmed to perfection on the unattached plywood panel before installation. Also, border decorating can be done before final assembly.

Getting started

Rip the frame members to width, then cut the deep rabbets. Follow with 45° miter cuts at the ends, then cut grooves for plywood splines at the corners with the aid of the jig in Photo 2.

If you own four miter clamps, use them to glue the frame together. Otherwise, work on a flat board and insert pieces of waxed paper under each corner to prevent gluing the frame to the work table. Clamp the end pieces directly to the work table, insert the sides with splines, then clamp in place with bar clamps.

Carefully sand off any residual glue before the next step: cutting the rabbet around the sides and back of the frame bottom. This is done with a dado head on a table saw. Use a wood facing strip on the saw fence to set the distance between the blade and the steel fence. This permits an inboard cut along the edge of the frame. A hold-down block clamped to the fence, directly over the blade center, will help to maintain proper contact throughout the run.

The ¾-in. plywood bottom panel is edged with

¾-in.-square strips of cherry, joined with blind dowels. Use the same setup for cutting the rabbets and dadoes as was used for the frame.

The front and back ends of the four cross members are faced with ⅛-in.-thick strips before the final assembly in order to conceal the end grain.

Screws—through the bottom—are used with glue to attach the back board and the four crosspieces. The frame gets glue only, no screws. *If the rabbet joints are well fitted,* glue alone will do the job. When the glue has dried, remove glue lumps and true up all surfaces with a belt sander.

Constructing the trestles

The trestles are assembled with blind dowels and glue. Mark the joint locations with a template of thin cardboard.

Use the miter gauge (or radial saw) to cut the top and bottom angles on the legs. The steep angles on the top insides of the legs can be cut on the radial saw with the arrangement shown in Photo 5. Or, make a wedge-shaped guide board to ride against the fence of the table saw.

Use a doweling jig to bore the holes for ⅜x2-in. spiral-grooved dowels. Sand all parts *before* assembly. Apply the glue sparingly and let it air-dry for a few minutes before bringing the parts together. This minimizes parts sliding about.

7 DOWELING jig assures true perpendicular holes and easier assembly.

8 USE paper shims to obtain slip fit when spacing trestle support cleats.

9 CUT ALL drawer fronts from same board to assure pleasing grain.

10 USE AUXILIARY fence with stops, molding-cutter to round drawer-top edge.

11 WITH ROUTER and template cutout, or chisel and mallet, cut recesses.

12 NYLON TAPE strips on cabinet drawers, replace drawer hardware.

Some say the best way to handle squeezed-out glue is to let it become almost dry, but *not* brittle. At this point, shave it off with a chisel.

Screw and glue the trestle-support cleats in place, using paper shims between the cross pieces and cleats to obtain accurate alignment for a slip fit.

The trestles are held together in matching pairs with two ¼-in. steel pegs; one end of each peg is secured with a drop of epoxy. If the desk needn't be portable, one screw in each cleat secures the trestles.

Building the drawers

First, cut the drawer fronts from a single board. Then, after cutting the other parts to size, run them over a dado head to form the rabbets and grooves. Run a stopped corner round on both sides of the top edges of the drawer sides. This can be done with a corner-round molding-cutter head on the table saw, with a strip of wood with stop blocks clamped to the saw fence, or with a router and rounding-over bit.

The drawer pulls are set into ⅜-in.-deep recesses routed into the drawer fronts. To use the same hardware, make the simple guide shown in Photo 11, from ¼-in. plywood or hardboard.

To assemble the drawers: Use finishing nails and glue to attach a drawer side to a front and a back. Apply glue to the grooves, then insert the bottom. Attach the second side, set nails and fill the holes.

Strips of nylon tape, used instead of conventional drawer-slides, give smooth, easy movement. Cut strips about 2 in. long and apply them to the rear bottom of the drawer sides and to the fronts of the drawer compartments.

Making the desktop

Cut ½-in. plywood to fit perfectly into the frame recess, with top surface 1/16 in. *below* the surface of the frame. The Naugahyde will make up the 1/16-in. difference.

The Naugahyde used for this project is available at fabric shops in 54-in. widths, so you'll need ⅔ yard. Be sure to specify Service Quality, which has the proper thickness.

Rough-trim it to overhang about 1 in. on all sides of the plywood. Apply contact adhesive to both surfaces and allow to dry. Naugahyde dries somewhat slowly, so apply the cement to the Naugahyde about a half hour before coating the wood. Use two sheets of wrapping paper as a separator while positioning the material on the wood. Slip out the first piece to allow partial contact, then slip out the other. Use the back of your hand to press the material gradually into place, working from the center outwards. Use a 3- or

INSTALLING THE 'LEATHER' TOP

1 USE contact cement to bond Naugahyde to wood; press outward.

2 ALCOHOL lamp, embossing tool, Mylar foil are used for decorative border.

3 AS PIECES of masking tape hold foil in place, butt ends of foil strips.

4 STRAIGHT wood strip guides stamp as you emboss first row of border.

5 SECOND ROW is made freehand. Hot stamp makes up to six impressions.

6 AFTER completing series of impressions, peel away foil.

7 APPLY GLUE with care, allowing it to set for 10 minutes before dropping in top and applying weight.

8 SOME OF the nails for hardware should be shortened so they don't collide when driven into top.

4-in. roller to assure complete contact.

Turn the panel over and use a very sharp knife to trim the Naugahyde flush with the edge of the plywood. The leftover larger piece of material should also be cemented to a scrap board for the next phase.

For the embossing you'll need an alcohol lamp, a decorative leathercraft stamp, a roll of 1-in.-wide Mylar gold foil and some masking tape. Use *only* alcohol to fuel the lamp. Other fuels,

and candles, can soil the work with soot. The stamp is available at hobby or leathercraft shops. To prevent finger burns, make a scrap-wood handle for the stamping tool.

Start by cutting and taping strips of the foil into place, dull side down. Do not overlap the corners; they must butt evenly without spaces. Apply the tape close to the edges so it won't be in the way of the design. The stamp design is crescent shaped, so a double impression, face to face,

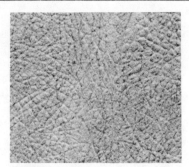

PLASTIC laminate has appearance of real leather.

LATEX contact adhesive is applied to both surfaces; let dry until clear.

ROUTER with laminate trimming bit is used to remove excess.

Leather-like laminate top

You may prefer a plastic laminate top in place of the Naugahyde. To apply it, first cut the sheet about ⅜-in. oversize on all sides to allow for trimming after bonding. Cut with a fine-toothed saw with little or no set. Next, apply contact cement to both surfaces and allow it to dry. Then bond plastic to the plywood, using Kraft paper as a separator while positioning the laminate.

The water-applied decals won't adhere properly to the textured surface unless you first apply sizing. To do so, brush on a coat of Aqua Podge or a similar latex-based decoupage finish. Allow to dry. Since arranging decals can be tricky, first lay them out in a dry run. Some designs may have to be cut to fit. Apply decals according to instructions, protect with paper and press firmly with a small rubber roller. When the decals have dried, apply another coat of decoupage finish over the top.

must be made to obtain the completed design. The first impression, which forms one half of the pattern, is made against a strip of wood which will assure obtaining a straight line of scallops. Tape the guide strip in place so it covers exactly half the foil's length.

The tool makes an impression 1 in. long. To end up with a full loop at the ends of a run, make pencil marks about 1 in. apart on the guide strip. Position the guide accordingly. If the inside cross borders don't divide evenly into full inches, you can make a partial impression by inserting a few sheets of paper between foil and stamp. Or, overlap each crescent slightly to make the pattern fit.

Heat the stamp for 10 or 15 seconds. Set up the scrap piece of Naugahyde with a strip of foil in place and make an impression by pressing the stamp squarely into it. If the tool is too hot it'll scorch both foil and the Naugahyde. Quickly make another test impression. If it looks good, make a series of impressions on the work. Position the tool so both points of the crescent butt up against the guide. Press down firmly and hold the tool in place for about one second each impression. Each heating of the tool should be sufficient for five or six impressions. Don't go beyond this, because an unheated tool will not transfer the gold. Make a test impression each time the tool is reheated.

When the initial row of scallops is completed, remove the guide strip and continue the embossing freehand by matching up the crescent points. When all the stamping is done, peel away the foil.

Finishing the desk

Apply the finish *before* installing the top. The prototype was stained with cherry satin stain, followed with two coats of clear satin finish. All nonexposed surfaces, including all parts of the drawers, were given a coat of sealer. Heavy staining frequently hides the beauty of wood. For a very light stain, first apply a very diluted coat of sanding sealer (1 part sealer, 5 parts thinner). Sand lightly with 220 paper, then stain.

To install the top, lay in a neat bead of glue, being careful to keep away from the top edges. Put top in place and weight with heavy books. Attach three sections of campaign hardware corners on the four top corners; two each at the lower corners. Note that the close proximity of the nails necessitates clipping some of them short, so they won't interfere with each other. Start the nail holes first, then withdraw and reinsert the clipped nails where necessary.

Rolltop desk for nostalgia buffs

■ BACK IN THE ERA of the trolley car and Model-T, the rolltop desk was popular in both home and office. Today, it's a cherished antique and you can pay as much as $1,300 and more for a store-bought reproduction. Build it yourself in fine cherry at a much lower cost for materials. Here's how:

Step-by-step construction

1. Rip the strips for all the frames: upper, lower and center. Use cherry where visible, poplar otherwise.

2. Cut tongues in ends of frame side members (use table saw with spacer between two outer blades of dado set to form two parallel cuts at same time). Tenonner or homemade jig should be used.

3. Cut ¼-in. grooves in all side and end frame members, ¼-in. deep. Cut dust covers from ¼-in. gum plywood. Make a bit scant to allow space for glue.

4. Cut the pedestal side panels to size from veneer plywood.

5. Use straightedge guide to cut veneer panels to exact size. Since pieces are too large to handle on the average table saw, a portable circular saw is the best. Use great care in setting up the guide and use a smooth-cutting blade. Cuts must be finish cuts. Note: Tack nails are okay for saw guide because all cutting must be done from the back surface of panel in order to obtain clean, sharp edges on the face of the panel with a portable saw.

6. Method of notching corners of front frame members to allow the installation of facing strips on the veneer side panels is optional: Do it with dado cutter or by adding ¼ x ¾-in. strips to the fronts. The strips are cut short at both ends and must be glued perfectly centered.

7. Use dado head to cut the four dado grooves in the four pedestal panels. Mark all panels for advantageous grain orientation and make each cut on each panel before repositioning rip fence.

8. Don't use white glue or aliphatics; both set too fast for assembling the pedestals. Plastic resin is okay because it allows about 25 minutes assembly time at 70° F. Scrape off all glue run-off with a sharp chisel; use damp cloth to remove traces that remain.

9. Glue edge strip to each bottom back frame to form groove for the back panel.

10. Use brads and glue to install pedestal back panels. Add solid cherry strips to raw plywood edges at back.

11. Cut pedestal base pieces to rough overall size, then miter corners carefully for perfect fit.

12. Attach long trim pieces to sides of pedestal first. If you prefer to avoid mitered corners, use butt joints at the corners and lap the side members with the fronts.

13. Cut front and rear base pieces, miter or butt the ends, and glue.

14. Nails driven from rear with only the points protruding will keep the base pieces in place during clamping—a very important step.

15. Fit the back apron "Q" so it sets in ¼ in. closer to the front than is indicated in the full-size

BLOCK CLAMPED to rule assures accurate straightedge placement to saw plywood.

GOOD SIDE of panel is placed down and panel is supported by 2x3s on sawhorses.

IDENTICAL DADO cuts are made before moving fence. Outboard work support is *must*.

TENON JIG and pair of same-size blades with spacer are used to cut frame tongues.

GROOVED END members are added to side-pieces after the latter are on dust panel.

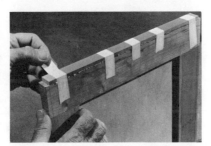

CORNER NOTCHES are formed by gluing short ¼-in.-thick strips to the front edges.

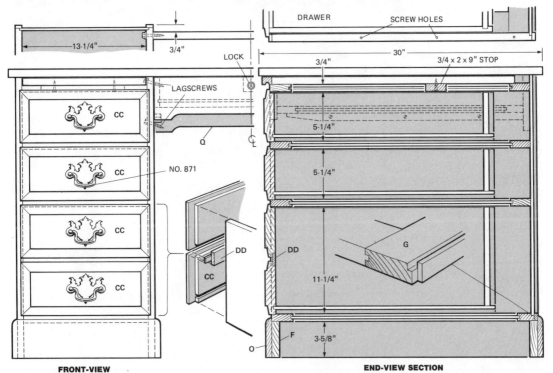

FRONT-VIEW   **END-VIEW SECTION**

USE A SLOW-SETTING resin glue rather than white to allow ample assembly time.

TOOTHPICK STANDOFFS keep tape away from glue line on inside pedestal surfaces.

CENTER FRAME is set in place without glue, then drilled for screw pilot holes.

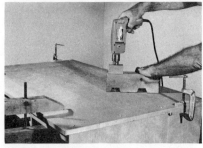

COUNTERBORED HOLES for wood plugs are drilled at right depth with homemade jig.

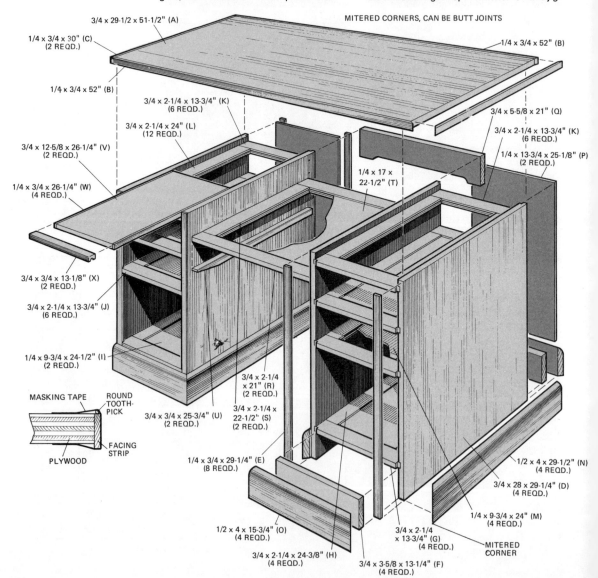

3/4 x 29-1/2 x 51-1/2" (A)

MITERED CORNERS, CAN BE BUTT JOINTS

1/4 x 3/4 x 30" (C)
(2 REQD.)

1/4 x 3/4 x 52" (B)

1/4 x 3/4 x 52" (B)

3/4 x 2-1/4 x 13-3/4" (K)
(6 REQD.)

3/4 x 2-1/4 x 24" (L)
(12 REQD.)

3/4 x 12-5/8 x 26-1/4" (V)
(2 REQD.)

1/4 x 3/4 x 26-1/4" (W)
(4 REQD.)

3/4 x 5-5/8 x 21" (Q)

3/4 x 2-1/4 x 13-3/4" (K)
(6 REQD.)

1/4 x 13-3/4 x 25-1/8" (P)
(2 REQD.)

1/4 x 17 x 22-1/2" (T)

3/4 x 3/4 x 13-1/8" (X)
(2 REQD.)

3/4 x 2-1/4 x 13-3/4" (J)
(6 REQD.)

1/4 x 9-3/4 x 24-1/2" (I)
(2 REQD.)

MASKING TAPE

ROUND TOOTH-PICK

FACING STRIP

PLYWOOD

3/4 x 3/4 x 25-3/4" (U)
(2 REQD.)

3/4 x 2-1/4 x 21" (R)
(2 REQD.)

3/4 x 2-1/4 x 22-1/2" (S)
(2 REQD.)

1/4 x 3/4 x 29-1/4" (E)
(8 REQD.)

1/2 x 4 x 29-1/2" (N)
(4 REQD.)

3/4 x 28 x 29-1/4" (D)
(4 REQD.)

1/4 x 9-3/4 x 24" (M)
(4 REQD.)

MITERED CORNER

1/2 x 4 x 15-3/4" (O)
(4 REQD.)

3/4 x 2-1/4 x 13-3/4" (G)
(4 REQD.)

3/4 x 2-1/4 x 24-3/8" (H)
(4 REQD.)

3/4 x 3-5/8 x 13-1/4" (F)
(4 REQD.)

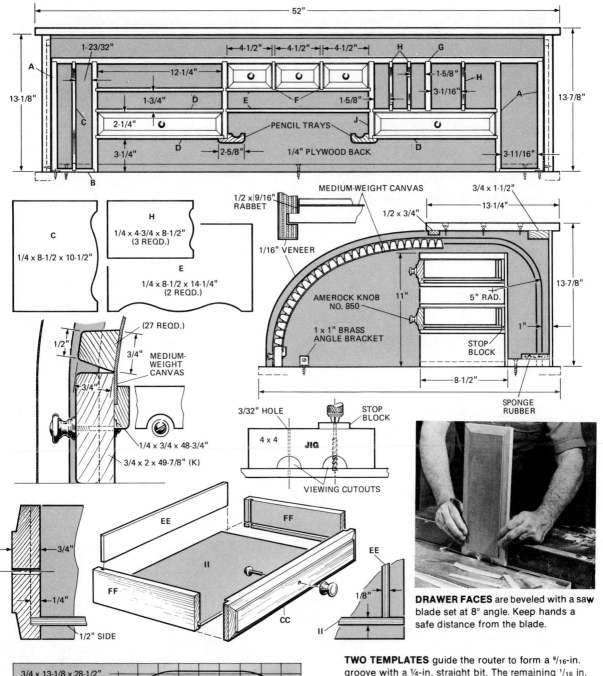

DRAWER FACES are beveled with a saw blade set at 8° angle. Keep hands a safe distance from the blade.

TWO TEMPLATES guide the router to form a $9/16$-in. groove with a ¼-in. straight bit. The remaining $1/16$ in. between the ¼-in. grooves is removed cleanly by carefully guiding your router freehand through the area.

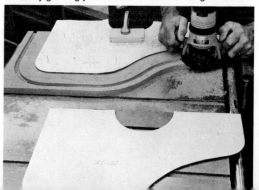

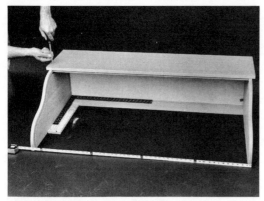

AFTER THE PARTS are test-fitted, screws are then driven in the counterbored holes and capped.

PENCIL TRAYS are made by passing the stock at a 75° angle across a 10-in. blade.

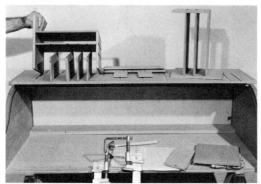

PREASSEMBLE THE RIGHT and left section of the cubbyhole unit first, then glue the rest.

BEVELED SLATS for tambour lid are ripped with a sharp blade tipped at a 10° angle.

SLATS ARE glued to the cloth back 8 to 10 at a time. Apply the glue carefully to the cloth only.

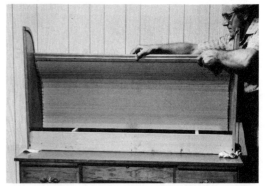

SLAT ENDS are waxed, then inserted into the track. Complete the project by screwing the top to the base.

plans. This is to allow clearance for direct drilling of lagscrew pilot holes from within the pedestal. This is an easier and more effective way to secure (rather than to use blind dowels as shown in plan). Use ¼ x 1½-in. hex-head lags and drive with socket wrench.

16. Screw and glue center frame supports into place.

17. Install center frame and drill holes for screws (instead of dowels) from within the base. Countersink the heads.

18. Use smooth-cutting blade to cut desktop

panel. Add ¼ x ¾-in. solid wood strips to ends, then front and rear strips to conceal edges.

19. If sufficient number of long clamps are not available to clamp the strips, you can do a good job with masking tape. Apply plenty of strips to insure good contact.

20. Important note when using tape to apply the vertical strips to the front edges of the pedestals: Elsewhere the strips are cut a bit oversize so they overhang and later are planed flush. But here the strips must be fitted flush at the start along the inner sides of the pedestals because they would be difficult to trim flush. In this case, it is advisable to use round toothpick standoffs to keep the tape away from the glue line. Otherwise, a gummy residue will result that's hard to remove.

21. When using masking tape, it is important to get a good-quality brand.

22. To drill holes for screws in desktop, set the top onto pedestals, then draw pencil lines on bottom of the top panel to outline the location of the pedestals.

23. Drill a ³⁄₃₂ in. pilot hole for each screw location. Do this from the back face using the pencil outline as a guide. Since the panel cannot be handled on the drill press, all drilling must be done by hand. Therefore a drilling jig is a must for accuracy.

Position top on pedestals

24. When preliminary pilot holes have been drilled through the top, position the top onto the pedestals and drill through the top to transfer the pilot holes into the top edges of the pedestals.

25. Use a spur bit (which has a brad point) to counterbore ³⁄₈-in. holes ⅛-in. deep into the top for matching wood plugs. Use the drilling jig for controlling depth and to assure perpendicularity.

26. Now proceed to drill the larger screw clearance holes into the top. Note that if the larger screw clearance holes were bored first, the spur bit would wobble around and tear up the work.

Steps for assembling

27. Glue and screw center frame and apron between pedestals. Apply glue to top edges and to the top and secure with screws. Be sure piece is level on floor or table.

28. Cut plugs from solid stock with a plug cutter—orient the grain direction and glue into place. Go easy with the glue.

29. Drawer fronts. Set the saw arbor to 8° bevel and slice ends first, then the sides; otherwise, chipping may occur. Pieces can be held firmly against rip fence by hand for this operation.

30. Rolltop. Plans call for ⁹⁄₁₆-in.-wide groove in the ends for the tambour top. The contoured groove is best cut with a router using a straight bit.

31. After gluing up solid stock to get 13⅛-in. width, bandsaw the contours, then prepare to cut the grooves.

32. A router bit which will cut a ⁹⁄₁₆-in.-wide groove in one pass is rare, if one exists at all, therefore, a ¼-in. bit is used—a common size.

Template from hardboard

33. A "twin" or two-part template cut from standard tempered hardboard is used to cut the grooves. The radii vary between the two parts of the template so great care must be exercised to make the templates.

34. Templates. Draw the pattern full size onto paper, including the dotted base lines. Rubber-cement the drawings onto hardboard and bandsaw them carefully. Note that the difference between both forms is ⁵⁄₁₆ in. and parallel. Tape both forms together with base lines lined up and with smaller form centered side to side over larger form; drill a couple of registration pilot holes for nails through both sections.

35. Center one of the templates onto the end panel with the base line even with the bottom edge of the stock. Drive in a pair of snug-fitting brads to hold in alignment. Clamp to work table and make the first pass with the router. Take off only a little at a time to avoid burning.

36. When depth is reached, remove the first template and install the other using the same nail pilot holes to assure exact lineup.

37. The two cuts made with the router will result in two ¼-in. grooves with a space of ¹⁄₁₆-in. from outside to outside; thus a narrow strip of waste will remain in the center of the groove. This is cleaned out by making a freehand pass with the router.

38. Use a carbide-tip tool for cutting the tambour grooves and make each pass about ⅛-in. or even less until ³⁄₈-in. depth is reached.

39. After the grooves are cut and the inner faces of the end panels sanded, the top and back are assembled. Counterbored screws are used to make glue contact of top to sides. Plug the holes.

40. Cubbyhole unit. Make the required dado cuts, then assemble the left and right sections. This will simplify assembly considerably. If an attempt is made to put it all together in one operation, proper clamping would be impossible. Half-inch lumber for this is not usually stocked so you'll have to have it surface-planed at a lumberyard.

41. Prestain and finish the face of the back panel, then put it aside and proceed to stain the compartments. The job is tough because your hands won't fit in some of the compartments. Work from both sides (thus the reason for leaving off the back). See finishing steps later.

42. Tambour lid. Cut some boards to the required length for the slats, then run a dado cutter over the ends to form the notch.

43. Use a smooth-cutting blade to cut the strips. Set the arbor for a 10° tilt, then run each piece through twice to obtain the required bevel on both sides. Use two push sticks for safety and accuracy.

Sand and stain carefully

44. Sand and apply the finish to each piece before assembly. Don't get stain on the bottom surface; otherwise glue will not adhere properly. Use a flat board for a work surface. Lay sheets of kitchen wax paper down to prevent accidental sticking to table. Tape the canvas to the table to keep it flat, then brush a coat of glue on canvas (not the wood). Work about 8 to 10 slats at a time. Most wood warps when cut into thin sections so it is practically impossible to control all the slats in one step. Use sufficient number of clamps to get ample pressure throughout. The use of a thin guide strip nailed to the table at one end will insure accurate alignment.

45. When tambour is dry, wax the ends, then insert into the grooves. Wax in the grooves will help. Screw the unit to the desktop.

46. Finishing. Presand all components before assembly, then final-sand by hand before applying finish. Use tack cloth to remove all sanding dust.

47. Apply a coat of lacquer thinned one to one with thinners to seal the wood and to permit better stain spread. Don't brush this on; use a pad of cheesecloth instead. Sand lightly after 10 minutes with fine paper (6/0); wipe with tack cloth.

48. Mix 1 part "antique walnut" and 1 part "concord cherry" stain. Apply with brush or cloth. Wipe off excess within 10 minutes.

49. When stain has dried (24 hours), apply a coat of low gloss wood finish. Sand first coat with 6/0 paper, then apply a second, final coat. Now stand back and admire your heirloom.

MATERIALS LIST
PEDESTAL BASE

Pcs.	Size (letter key to drawings), description
1	¾ x 29½ x 51½" (A) Top*
2	¼ x ¾ x 52" (B) Top edge strips, long
2	¼ x ¾ x 30" (C) Top edge strips, short
4	¾ x 28 x 29¼" (D) Pedestal sides*
8	¼ x ¾ x 29¼" (E) Pedestal facing strips
4	¾ x 3⅝ x 13¼" (F) Bottom rails front and back*
4	¾ x 2¼ x 13¾" (G) Bottom frames front and back
4	¾ x 2¼ x 24⅜" (H) Bottom frames, sides*
2	¼ x 9¾ x 24½" (I) Dust panels***
6	¾ x 2¼ x 13¾" (J) Upper frames, fronts
6	¾ x 2¼ x 13¾" (K) Upper frames, backs*
12	¾ x 2¼ x 24" (L) Upper frames, sides*
4	¼ x 9¾ x 24" (M) Dust panels***
4	½ x 4 x 29½" (N) Pedestal base, long
4	½ x 4 x 15¾" (O) Pedestal base, short
2	¼ x 13¾ x 25⅛" (P) Pedestal backs***
1	¾ x 5⅝ x 21" (Q) Back apron
2	¾ x 2¼ x 21" (R) Center frame, front and back*
2	¾ x 2¼ x 22½" (S) Center frame, sides*
1	¼ x 17 x 22½" (T) Dust panel***
2	¾ x ¾ x 25¾" (U) Center frame supports*
2	¾ x 12⅝ x 26¼" (V) Drawboards**
4	¼ x ¾ x 26¼" (W) Drawboard edge strips
2	¾ x ¾ x 13⅛" (X) Drawboard nosings
1	¾ x 4 7/16 x 20⅞" (Y) Center drawer, front
1	½ x 2 7/16 x 20⅜" (Z) Center drawer, back*
2	½ x 3 3/16 x 23½" (AA) Center drawer, sides*
1	¼ x 20⅜ x 23⅜" (BB) Center drawer, bottom***
8	¾ x 5½ x 13¾" (CC) Drawer fronts
2	½ x 1¼ x 13¾" (DD) File-drawer front joiners
4	½ x 4 7/16 x 12⅝" (EE) Drawer backs*
8	½ x 5 3/16 x 23¾" (FF) Drawer sides*
2	½ x 10⅜ x 12⅝" (GG) File drawer, backs*
4	½ x 11 3/16 x 23¾" (HH) File drawer, sides*
6	¼ x 12⅝ x 23⅝" (II) Drawer bottoms***
2	¾ x 2 x 9" (JJ) Drawer board stops*
8	Drawer pulls

Tambour top

Pcs.	Size (letter key to drawings), description
1	Lock
1	¾ x 13¼ x 52" Top
1	¾ x 1⅝ x 49" Top back rail*
1	½ x ¾ x 49" Top front strip
1	¾ x 4⅛ x 49" Bottom rail*
2	¾ x 13⅛ x 28½" Ends**
1	¼ x 13⅛ x 49¾" Back***
1	¾ x 2 x 49⅝" Bottom slat (K)
27	¾ x ¾ x 49⅝" Tambour strips
1	¼ x ¾ x 48¾" Canvas cover strip

Interior of tambour top

1	½ x 8½ x 48⅞"
4	½ x 8½ x 10⅝" (A) Panels
2	¼ x 3 15/16 x 8½" (B) Bottoms
1	¼ x 8½ x 10½" (C) Scrolled divider
5	¼ x 8½ x 12½" (D) Panels
2	¼ x 8½ x 14¼" (E) Panels
2	¼ x 2¾ x 8½" (F) Partitions
1	½ x 4¾ x 8½" (G) Partition
3	¼ x 4¾ x 8½" (H) Scrolled dividers
2	½ x 7⅜ x 8½" (J) Partitions
2	¾ x 2⅝ x 8½" Pencil troughs
1	¼ x 11 x 48⅞" Back***
3	½ x 2 7/16 x 4 7/16" Drawer fronts
3	⅛ x 2 1/16 x 4 3/16" Drawer backs
6	¼ x 2 7/16 x 8 3/16" Drawer sides
3	⅛ x 4 3/16 x 8 3/16" Drawer bottoms
2	½ x 2 3/16 x 12⅛" Drawer fronts
2	⅛ x 1 13/16 x 11⅞" Drawer backs
4	¼ x 2 3/16 x 8 3/16" Drawer sides
2	⅛ x 11⅞ x 8 3/16" Drawer bottoms
7	⅛ x ½ x 1" Drawer stops
7	Amerock knobs No. 850
1	21 x 48¾" Medium-weight canvas

* Poplar wood
** Veneer plywood (cherry)
*** Plywood (gum)

Wall-hung study center

■ IF YOU CAN SAW a board, you can build this wall-hung study center, for that's just about all you have to do to make it. You start out with plain flat boards and simply saw them to length, without even touching the width. The important thing is to saw the ends square.

Design the project around standard-size boards that any lumberyard sells. This will not only give you the ultimate in simplified construction, but will create a handsome, functional piece that any member of your family would be glad to have.

The unit provides an off-the-floor desk with a shelf below, a cork pinup board for displaying star-studded papers, roomy shelves for reference books and a cupboard for storing those treasures all children collect. Pegs provide a place to hang toys. There's even a bin to corral stray toys.

Remember that a 1 x 12 board, for example, is not a full 1 in. thick and 12 in. wide, but actually measures ¾ x 11½ in. This is true of all dimensioned lumber. Actual measurement is less than stock size.

Any solid lumber of the western pine species, such as ponderosa pine, larch or white fir, is appropriate. A natural finish (protected by a clear sealer), combined with painted cupboard doors and a colorful plastic desktop, will give it eye appeal.

Nails are used to fasten the 9-ft. 1x12s to the vertical members, and they are also used when nailing the desk compartment together. All the rest of the pieces are joined with 1½-in. No. 10 oval-head screws, which are first seated in chrome cup washers and inserted in predrilled holes in the wood. The three adjustable cupboard shelves rest on regular shelf standards and supports. Six 2½-in. toggle bolts are used to hang the unit.

AFTER HORIZONTAL boards are nailed to verticals, all permanent shelves are installed with screws.

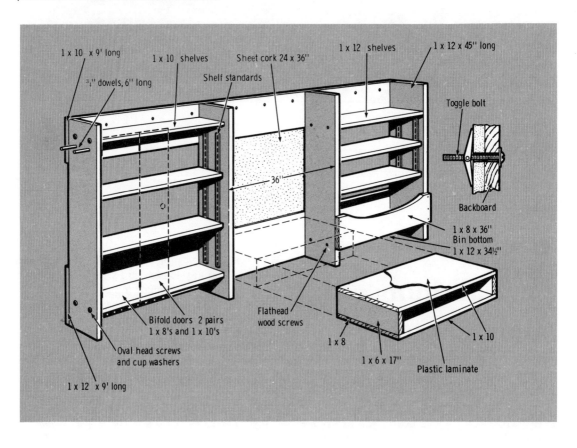

Dining room set

■ THIS CHARMING dining set can be built for about one-fifth the cost of a retail store version of comparable quality.

Southern (soft) maple is used for all but the tabletop, which is made of ¾-in. birch-veneer, lumber-core plywood and edged with solid maple to achieve a thick look. The coloring and grain patterns of these woods are look-alikes so they can be readily intermixed. Use birch veneer for the top because you'll find that maple veneer plywood is not commonly available at most lumberyards.

If you haven't worked with southern maple, you're in for a treat. It tools nicely, and while it's known as a "soft" wood, it is more than hard enough for furniture-making.

The table, a modernized version of the trestle style, is not difficult to construct. The cross rail (stretcher) utilizes blind mortise-and-tenon joints and the leg members are put together with cross-lap joints held only with glue.

You shouldn't have trouble making the comfortable swivel chairs. We "engineered" their construction so you can build them with minimal fuss and bother. Note how the turning blanks for the pedestals are made up with 2⅜-in. preformed notches, which would be practically impossible to make with any degree of accuracy or safety *after* the pedestals are turned. Also, rather than call for a steam-bent curved chair back, you can use a segmented glued block to obtain a strong parallel-grain structure throughout the curve.

Steps for making the table

1. Start with the understructure. Cut the ⁵⁄₄ (1⅛-in.) stock for uprights and cross members to size and plane them smooth on the jointer before cutting the cross-lap joints. Removal of stock along the edges after the joints have been made would loosen them.

2. The blind mortise-and-tenon joints for the cross-rail stretcher are next. Form tenons in the rail by making a partial saw cut completely around each end, then remove the waste with a dado head. Then bore a series of holes part way

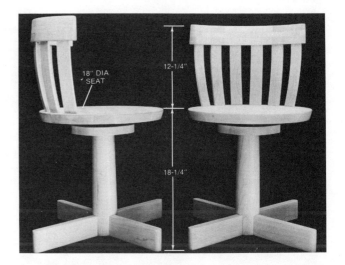

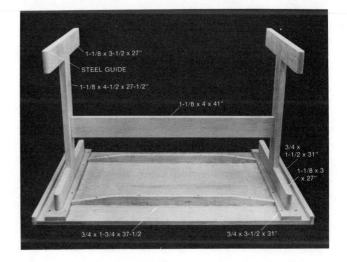

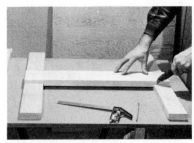

POSITION upright on base, and mark mating half-lap with knife.

MAKE BLIND cross-rail mortises by boring holes and chiseling out waste.

MAKE REPEATED passes to clear waste after making outside cuts halfway.

MOUNT GLUED-UP pedestal between lathe centers for turning.

APPLY GLUE and tighten lagscrews to secure base to pedestal. Add swivel.

USE HEADLESS brads for slip-proof alignment when clamping chair seats.

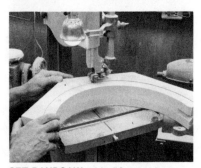

SET BANDSAW table 5°, use sharp blade, saw chair rail slowly.

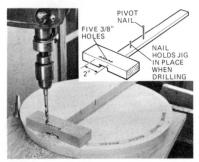

LINE UP slat mortises with pivoting jig and use it to drill series of holes.

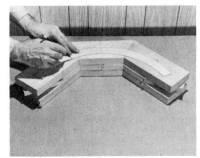

PLACE CARDBOARD template on bottom of back rail; trace for bandsawing.

into the leg members to rough-form the mortise—making sure the drill point does not go through the board—and clear out waste between the holes with a chisel.

3. Finish-sand the parts, then assemble the legs and cross members. When the glue has set, glue and screw the two ¾ x 3½ x 31-in. table-attaching cleats to the tops of both leg sections with 2-in. No. 10 fh screws.

4. Set the tabletop upside down on a pair of horses or other supports and check the surface with a level in both directions. If necessary, shim up the horses to adjust until the top lies perfectly plane. This is important—if the table is glue-assembled while uneven, you may possibly build in some unwanted twists.

5. Screw one of the assembled legs to the top with 1½-in. No. 10 fh screws in predrilled countersunk holes. Insert the cross rail, secure it with a pair of bar clamps, then screw the other leg assembly to the tabletop. Screw and glue the pair of stiffeners in place.

6. Use concealed nails with heads cut off to help align the mitered edge-facing strips. Install the end strips, glue and clamp. Follow with sides. Round the corners with a block plane, then sand the top.

Steps for making chairs

1. Cut a deep notch halfway through each piece of the chair bases to form the cross-lap joints. Round the ends on a stationary disc

CUT FOUR-WAY pedestal notch before gluing. Set blade high, make two cuts.

JIGSAW WASTE from between saw cuts in two outside members of group.

TEST NOTCHES for fit over base before gluing and clamping pieces.

CLAMPED crosspieces keep others flat. Wax paper prevents sticking.

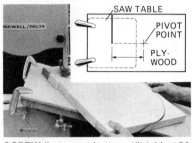

SCREW jig to seat bottom, tilt table 15° to cut perfect 18-in.-diameter.

FORM SLAT mortises by squaring up rows of holes in seat bottom with chisel.

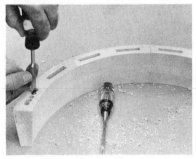

CUT MORTISES in chair-back rail as in seat. Drill holes with brad-point bit.

BANDSAW CURVED slats from solid stock, then drum-sand smooth.

USE TOP RAIL dry (no glue) to hold glued lower ends of slats in alignment.

sander, then glue the members to form the crossed base.

2. Select three lengths of stock to form the turning blanks for each pedestal. Notch the ends of the two outer pieces so they will slide freely over the 1⅛ x 2⅞-in. base section. Insert a few concealed nails without heads for registration, then sandwich the three pieces together. Mark each blank for later match-up with its base. Remove excess glue inside the notches to insure a good fit later.

3. When both blanks have been made up, glue a scrap of hardwood to the notched ends for mounting in the lathe. Bandsaw the four waste corners from the blocks to save a lot of rough lathe work.

4. Use the gouge and skew to turn the slightly tapered cylinder to shape, and use the parting tool at the top to cut the pedestal to proper length. The block at the bottom is cut off by bandsawing at the glue line.

5. The chair seat is next. Select seven lengths of ¾ (1⅜-in.) stock to make up the seat. Check your rip saw to be sure it is cutting perfectly square. Lay out the pieces so that the annual rings alternately curve up and down. This will counteract any warping tendency. Insert headless brads into predrilled holes so the points protrude about ¼ in. Working on a flat surface, proceed to press the pieces together to form registration brad holes. Separate the pieces, apply glue, then clamp together in this manner: Tape kitchen wax paper

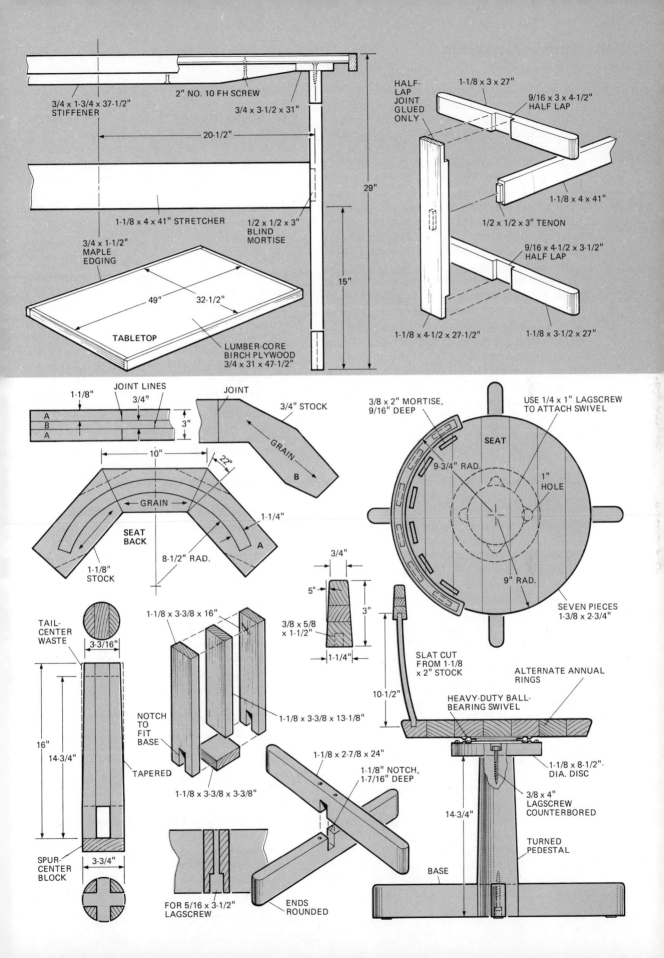

3/4 x 1-3/4 x 37-1/2" STIFFENER

2" NO. 10 FH SCREW

3/4 x 3-1/2 x 31"

20-1/2"

29"

1-1/8 x 4 x 41" STRETCHER

1/2 x 1/2 x 3" BLIND MORTISE

15"

3/4 x 1-1/2" MAPLE EDGING

49" 32-1/2"

TABLETOP

LUMBER-CORE BIRCH PLYWOOD 3/4 x 31 x 47-1/2"

HALF-LAP JOINT GLUED ONLY

1-1/8 x 3 x 27"

9/16 x 3 x 4-1/2" HALF LAP

1-1/8 x 4 x 41"

1/2 x 1/2 x 3" TENON

9/16 x 4-1/2 x 3-1/2" HALF LAP

1-1/8 x 4-1/2 x 27-1/2"

1-1/8 x 3-1/2 x 27"

1-1/8" 3/4"

JOINT LINES

A
B
A

3"

JOINT

3/4" STOCK

3/8 x 2" MORTISE, 9/16" DEEP

USE 1/4 x 1" LAGSCREW TO ATTACH SWIVEL

GRAIN

B

10" 22°

SEAT

9-3/4" RAD.

1" HOLE

GRAIN

SEAT BACK

1-1/4"

A

8-1/2" RAD.

1-1/8" STOCK

9" RAD.

3/4"

SEVEN PIECES 1-3/8 x 2-3/4"

5°

3"

3/8 x 5/8 x 1-1/2"

1-1/4"

TAIL-CENTER WASTE

3-3/16"

1-1/8 x 3-3/8 x 16"

SLAT CUT FROM 1-1/8 x 2" STOCK

10-1/2"

ALTERNATE ANNUAL RINGS

HEAVY-DUTY BALL-BEARING SWIVEL

16"

14-3/4"

NOTCH TO FIT BASE

1-1/8 x 3-3/8 x 13-1/8"

TAPERED

1-1/8 x 3-3/8 x 3-3/8"

1-1/8 x 2-7/8 x 24"

1-1/8" NOTCH, 1-7/16" DEEP

1-1/8 x 8-1/2"- DIA. DISC

3/8 x 4" LAGSCREW COUNTERBORED

14-3/4"

TURNED PEDESTAL

SPUR-CENTER BLOCK

3-3/4"

FOR 5/16 x 3-1/2" LAGSCREW

ENDS ROUNDED

BASE

to four scrap boards and clamp them to both sides of the bundle using moderate pressure. Apply bar clamps to pull the seven members together. Check that the whole thing is perfectly flat. If necessary, apply more pressure to the clamps on the line-up blocks.

6. The beveled 18-in.-diameter seat is easily cut with a simple circle-cutting jig on the bandsaw. Clamp a board with a partial cut through it (for blade entry) to the saw table. Drive a screw through the bottom of the board so that it is exactly 9 in. from the blade and in perfect alignment with the front edge of the blade teeth. This is very important because if the pivot point is ahead of or behind the teeth, the cut will be eccentric and the work will be spoiled.

You can test the right-angle alignment by trying the cut on some scrap cardboard. When ready, tilt the saw table 15°, start the cut freehand to get the blade into the wood, then stop the saw, insert the screw into the bottom of the seat to provide a pivot.

Cut slats freehand

7. The curved slats are cut from 5/4 (1⅛-in.) stock, freehand on the bandsaw. Sanding out the saw marks is easy if you use a 3-in. sanding drum on the drill press. Clamp a scrap of wood on edge and aim it to the center of the drum with just enough space to allow the work to pass through with a snug fit. Keep the work continuously perpendicular to the guide as you push it through. When all the insides have been sanded, move the guide a fraction closer and repeat the operation on the opposite side of the slats. Note that the bottom ends of the slats have a straight portion—be careful not to round them off. Some hand sanding will be required near the flats.

8. The curved back is made up by gluing eight angled segments together. A sandwich is made by stacking three, two and then another set of three blocks, one atop the other. This allows the grain to run as closely as possible in the direction of the curve. The alternating vertical joint lines produce a strong block.

9. The back is tapered in cross section so that it is wider at the bottom. Trace the outline of the bottom curves in the block. Set bandsaw table for a 5° bevel and make both cuts.

10. A simple hole-locating jig is used to bore a series of five overlapping holes in a straight line to form the mortises for the slats. The jig is made to pivot by driving a nail through the stick into the seat center. When the block is positioned

where required, a second nail is tacked into the stick to keep the block from moving. A ⅜-in. drill bit is driven through each hole in the block. Work with a spur bit for best results.

11. Use a chisel to clean out the waste and trim the mortises. Because of its shape, the curved back piece does not lend itself so readily to a jig for boring the holes for the mortises. Therefore these holes are lined up and drilled freehand. A slight error here can be tolerated— not so on the seat.

12. When all parts are sanded to completion, test the fit, then apply glue only to bottom ends of the slats and the seat mortises. The curved back is inserted, dry, only to help hold the parts in alignment. When the slats have been glued to the seat, you can proceed to apply glue to the backs. Work upside down, with the curved back resting on a table and the seat elevated and supported on a level plane. Gluing the back in two phases will prevent a messy glue runoff which could drip all over the slats.

Putting together the chair

13. Assembly of the chair: First use a hex-head lagscrew and glue to attach the ball-bearing support disc to the top of the pedestal. The hole must be counterbored so the screwhead doesn't project above the surface. Before attaching the disc, bore a 1-in. screw access hole properly located in the block.

Turn the unit over, apply glue and insert the base into the notches in the pedestal. Secure with four hexhead lags. Be sure to counterbore a hole large enough to receive a socket wrench which is required to turn the screws. Attach the swivel mechanism to the disc with lagscrews, then screw the upper section of the swivel to the seat bottom.

The screws are inserted one at a time through the 1-in. access hole in the block which is alternately rotated to reveal each screw-mounting hole.

14. Finish is optional. It might be refreshing to depart from the usual routine of staining the piece so you can apply a coat of sanding sealer followed with two coats of clear satin finish to obtain an interesting high-key effect.

15. Install four steel glides to both table and chair bases.

Seat covers are optional. Shown are oversize shag toilet-lid covers. Cut cardboard and 1-in.-thick-foam pieces to fit each seat 1 in. shy all around. Insert foam and then cardboard to retain shape of the cushions.

Trestle table

■ SERVING SIX PEOPLE comfortably, as well as offering the rugged good looks of Early American pine furniture, this hand-pegged, trestle dining table is a period piece you'll use and admire for years to come. Its beauty lies in its simplicity, both in design and construction. Best of all, it's made of common clear pine, which means you can get the wood to make it at any lumberyard.

Except for size, the two trestle benches are duplicates of the table, the main difference being the number of pieces required to build up the 30-in. wide top. The 1½-in.-thick stock, which is used for the table and benchtops, is doweled and glued together edgewise, then clamped. When the glue is

TABLETOP AND BENCHTOPS are made of clear-pine 2x8s doweled and edge-glued. Pegged stretchers add a great deal of rigidity to the table and benches.

dry, top surfaces of the built-up members are planed smooth, sanded with a medium-abrasive belt on a belt sander, or by hand, and then the top edges are rounded.

The leg patterns for benches and table are similar, and all six legs are sabre-sawed from 1⅛-in.-thick pine. Some lumberyards have 1⅛-in. pine 14 in. wide. Where you can't obtain this width, the stock for the table legs will have to be doweled and glued up like the tabletop. The open mortises in the legs are made 1⅛ in. wide to accept the shouldered ends of the stretchers. The

mortises are easily cut with a sabre saw by first boring a ½-in. hole for the saw blade. Cleat and foot members are cut to the sizes given and are attached to the scroll-cut legs with ½-in. dowels. Counterbored holes in the cleats permit husky screws to be used to anchor the legs to the table and benchtops.

A ¼ x 1-in. open mortise is made vertically in the stretcher tenons for ¼-in. tapered wedges. The mortises are located at a point which will draw the tenon shoulders tightly against the leg when the wedges are tapped in place.

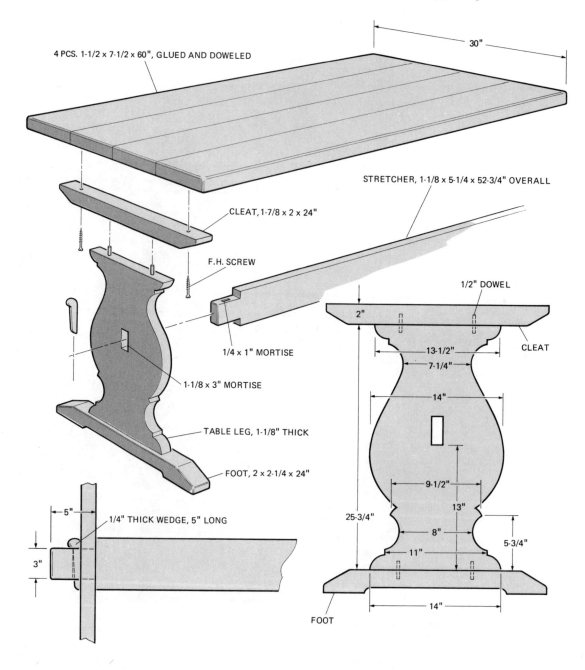

4 PCS. 1-1/2 x 7-1/2 x 60", GLUED AND DOWELED

30"

STRETCHER, 1-1/8 x 5-1/4 x 52-3/4" OVERALL

CLEAT, 1-7/8 x 2 x 24"

F.H. SCREW

1/4 x 1" MORTISE

1-1/8 x 3" MORTISE

TABLE LEG, 1-1/8" THICK

FOOT, 2 x 2-1/4 x 24"

5"

1/4" THICK WEDGE, 5" LONG

3"

1/2" DOWEL

2"

CLEAT

13-1/2"

7-1/4"

14"

9-1/2"

13"

8"

11"

5-3/4"

25-3/4"

14"

FOOT

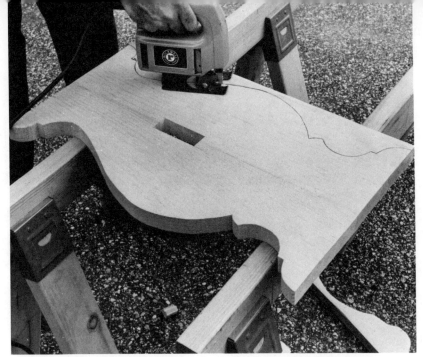

SABRE SAW makes quick work of sawing scrolled table and bench legs. Feed the saw slowly, follow the lines closely, then sand the edges with abrasive blocks.

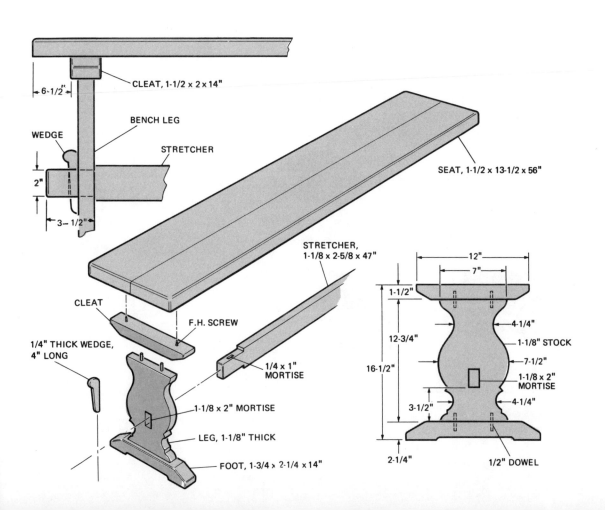

CLEAT, 1-1/2 x 2 x 14"

6-1/2"

WEDGE

BENCH LEG

STRETCHER

2"

3-1/2"

SEAT, 1-1/2 x 13-1/2 x 56"

STRETCHER, 1-1/8 x 2-5/8 x 47"

CLEAT

F.H. SCREW

1/4" THICK WEDGE, 4" LONG

1/4 x 1" MORTISE

1-1/8 x 2" MORTISE

LEG, 1-1/8" THICK

FOOT, 1-3/4 x 2-1/4 x 14"

12"

7"

1-1/2"

12-3/4"

16-1/2"

3-1/2"

2-1/4"

4-1/4"

1-1/8" STOCK

7-1/2"

1-1/8 x 2" MORTISE

4-1/4"

1/2" DOWEL

Classic oaken table

■ THERE'S SOMETHING REASSURING about eating at a sturdy oak table that you know will be around awhile. Our prototype, crafted from substantial red oak, should last a few lifetimes. The design is at home with almost any decor—traditional or contemporary—and it's functional. It can gracefully accommodate a bois-

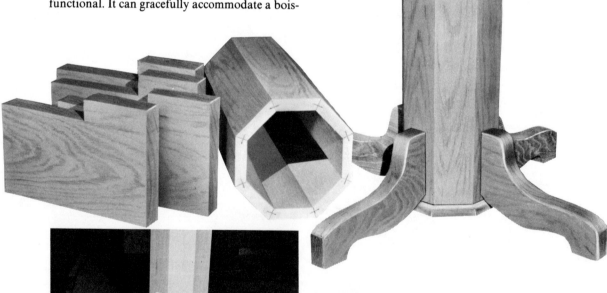

SPLINES REINFORCE pedestal's cooper joinery and insure a sturdy table support.

HANGER BOLTS turned into feet will be fastened to pedestal with nuts, washers. Stem-type casters are used.

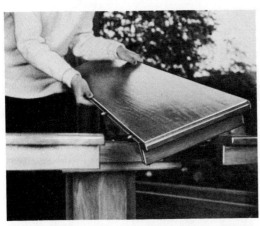

PINS IN EDGE of the extension leaf make it impossible to install leaf incorrectly. It's a one-person job.

terous holiday party or a quiet candlelit tête-a-tête, along with every meal in between.

Taken one step at a time, the table construction is easier than you would think. We give you all the details for making a circle-cutting jig, which not only simplifies cutting the tabletop and round apron in this project, but will come in handy for circle-cutting tasks in the future.

After gathering all materials, lay out and cut eight pedestal segments (A) with a table saw. Spline grooves can be cut with a saw blade having a ⅛-in. set. Use ⅛-in. hardwood plywood to make strong splines (J). Run through the assembly dry before gluing and clamping the joints. Belt clamps are ideal, but if you have none, loop ropes around the pedestal, then twist and secure them to serve as clamps.

Making the feet

Next, make a pattern for the table feet (G), using the grid in the plans. Trace the shape onto the glued-up oak stock and make the cuts with a bandsaw or heavy-duty sabre saw. Bore holes in the feet as directed by the caster manufacturer. Also bore corresponding pairs of holes in the feet tops and pedestal to accommodate the hanger bolts, which serve to join the two together.

Install the feet and complete the oak table support by making the octagonal base cap (B) and the top cap or slide support (E). Shape the detail around the base cap sides with a ⅜-in. rounding-over bit and use screws to fasten it to the column base. Use hanger bolts to fasten the slide support to the column top.

Carriage bolts can be used to attach the extension slides (L) to the slide support (H). Be sure to counterbore, so that bolt heads don't interfere with spreading and closing tabletop halves.

Making tabletop sections

All that remains is to make the tabletop sections and apron. Edge-join the boards (D) for the table halves.

Alternate the end-grain directions to help minimize warping, and strengthen the edge joints with dowels. After the boards have been glued and clamped, make the circle-cutting jig shown in the plans. For a simpler, nonadjustable version, use a nail as a fixed pivot pin. Locate the nail/pivot on the sliding-jig base 21 in. from the table-saw blade for cutting the semicircular aprons.

Now, secure the workpiece to the jig, using screws or nails driven up through part CC. (Do not install fasteners in line of cut.) Position the sliding jig base in the miter groove and align pivot pin on sliding base with hole in jig part CC. Adjust the blade height to ⅛ in. above the workpiece top surface and turn on the saw. Make straight cuts, removing a small amount of waste on each pass. Rotate the workpiece before—not during—each pass. Eventually you get a perfect half circle. Clean up rough spots with a belt sander.

Building apron assemblies

To make apron assemblies for the half-circle tops, assemble sections (F) on jig part CC to facilitate gluing and clamping. Once again, you can use band clamps, or rope twisted and secured to provide pressure. Use of spreader (EE), along with jig stop (DD), keeps assembly from collapsing while you set clamps or rope.

After the apron sections are glued, fasten them to the jig with nails from the underside of part CC. Cut to round using same procedure explained above.

Leaves with aprons, pins

Before the final assembly, make the table leaves with aprons to match those on the half-circle tabletops. Lay out and bore holes for ⅜-in.-dia. table pins and corresponding holes for the pins. Then install the tabletop lock and metal clips that keep the tops flush.

Apply stain of your choice following instructions on the can. Let dry 24 hours and apply paste wood filler (to fill the open pores). If necessary, tint filler with the stain. Let filler dry until shine disappears; then rub off with a coarse cloth (burlap). When dry, seal with a coat of thinned shellac and finish with a semigloss varnish.

GLUE UP the stock for the tabletop using dowels. Be sure to alternate grain to minimize warp.

USE JIG that is detailed in plans to cut a perfect circle with the table saw.

MATERIALS LIST—OAK TABLE

Key	Pcs.	Size and description
A	8	$^{13}/_{16}$ x $3^{7}/_{8}$ x 20" red oak
B	1	$^{13}/_{16}$ x 11 x 11" red oak
C	2	$^{13}/_{16}$ x $11^{1}/_{2}$ x 42" red oak
D	6	$^{13}/_{16}$ x 7 x 42" (max.) red oak
E	4	$^{13}/_{16}$ x 2 x $11^{1}/_{2}$" red oak
F	8	2 x $2^{1}/_{4}$ x $16^{5}/_{8}$" red oak
G	4	2 x 9 x 14" (may be glued-up) red oak
H	1	$^{3}/_{4}$ x 16 x 18" plywood
I	6	$^{1}/_{2}$ x 2 x $2^{1}/_{2}$" red oak
J	8	$^{1}/_{8}$ x 1 x 20" hardwood plywood
K	24	$^{3}/_{8}$"-dia. x 2" birch dowels
L	1	28" long (closed) extension slide set*
M	6	16-ga. x $^{3}/_{4}$ x $2^{1}/_{4}$" steel
N	16	birch table pins*
O	1	table lock*
P	4	2"-dia. casters
Q	8	$^{5}/_{16}$"-dia. x 3" hanger bolt*, nut, washer nut
R	4	$^{5}/_{16}$"-dia. x 3" carriage bolt, washer
S	4	No. 12 x 2" fh screws
T	24	No. 12 x $2^{1}/_{2}$" fh screws
U	8	No. 12 x $2^{1}/_{2}$" fh screws

MATERIALS LIST—CIRCLE-CUTTING JIG

Key	Pcs.	Size and description
V	14	No. 8 x $^{1}/_{2}$" fh screws
W	2	$^{1}/_{8}$ x $^{3}/_{4}$ x 24" tempered hardboard
X	1	$^{1}/_{2}$ x 12" chest slide support, or cut 16-gauge steel bar to suit
Y	1	$^{1}/_{4}$" length cut from nail
Z	1	$^{3}/_{16}$ x $^{5}/_{8}$" stovebolt and teenut
AA	1	$^{3}/_{4}$ x 20 x 24" plywood
BB	1	$^{1}/_{2}$ x $^{3}/_{4}$ x 22" hardwood miter bar
CC	1	$^{1}/_{4}$ x 24 x 42" plywood
DD	1	$^{3}/_{4}$ x 3 x 42" plywood
EE	1	2 x 2 x 40" (trim to fit)
FF	12	No. 6 x 1" fh screws

Misc.: White glue, $^{3}/_{4}$" brads to suit

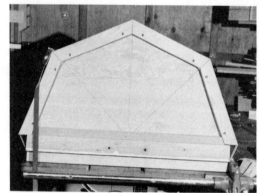

APRON SEGMENTS are splined and glued together. Then they are nailed to jig surface, CC.

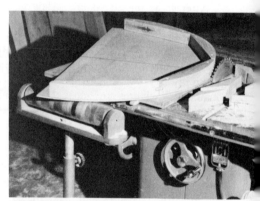

WITH APRON assembly on the sliding jig base, straight cuts on the table saw form a half circle.

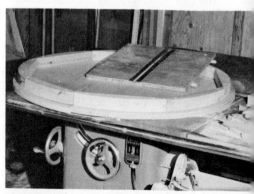

SLIDING JIG base can be used on other projects since it will cut many different sizes.

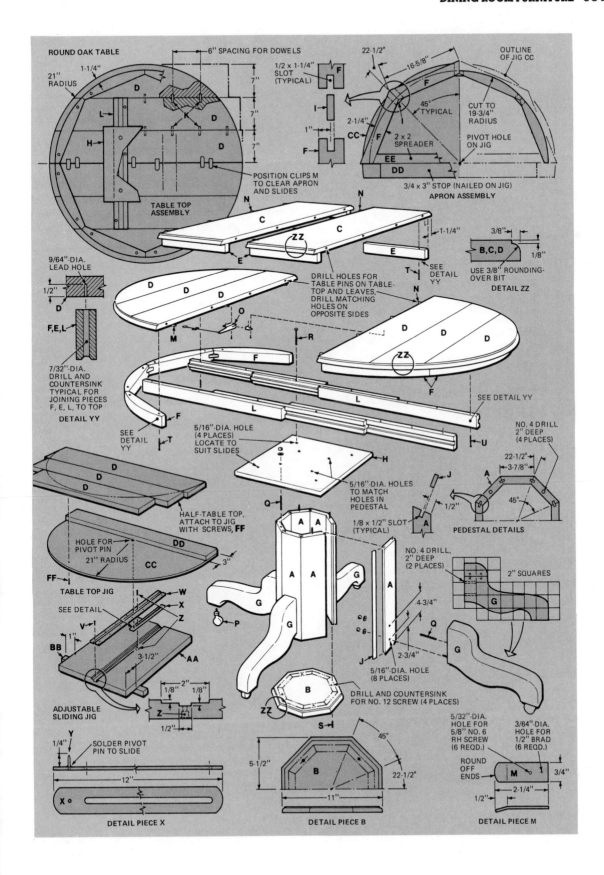

ROUND OAK TABLE

21" RADIUS

1-1/4"

6" SPACING FOR DOWELS

7"

7"

7"

POSITION CLIPS M TO CLEAR APRON AND SLIDES

TABLE TOP ASSEMBLY

1/2 x 1-1/4" SLOT (TYPICAL)

F

I

2-1/4"

1"

F

CC

F

22-1/2°

16-5/8"

45° TYPICAL

2 x 2 SPREADER

OUTLINE OF JIG CC

CUT TO 19-3/4" RADIUS

PIVOT HOLE ON JIG

EE

DD

3/4 x 3" STOP (NAILED ON JIG)

APRON ASSEMBLY

N

N

C

C

C

ZZ

E

E

1-1/4"

SEE DETAIL YY

T

N

3/8"

B,C,D

1/8"

USE 3/8" ROUNDING-OVER BIT

DETAIL ZZ

9/64"-DIA. LEAD HOLE

1/2"

D

D

F,E,L

7/32"-DIA. DRILL AND COUNTERSINK TYPICAL FOR JOINING PIECES F, E, L, TO TOP

DETAIL YY

SEE DETAIL YY

F

T

D

D

D

O

M

R

DRILL HOLES FOR TABLE PINS ON TABLE-TOP AND LEAVES, DRILL MATCHING HOLES ON OPPOSITE SIDES

D

D

D

ZZ

F

F

SEE DETAIL YY

F

L

L

U

NO. 4 DRILL 2" DEEP (4 PLACES)

D

D

D

HALF-TABLE TOP, ATTACH TO JIG WITH SCREWS, FF

5/16"-DIA. HOLE (4 PLACES) LOCATE TO SUIT SLIDES

H

Q

5/16"-DIA. HOLES TO MATCH HOLES IN PEDESTAL

J

1/2"

A

A

22-1/2°

3-7/8"

45°

PEDESTAL DETAILS

HOLE FOR PIVOT PIN

21" RADIUS

CC

DD

3"

FF

TABLE TOP JIG

SEE DETAIL

W

X

Z

V

1"

BB

3-1/2"

AA

ADJUSTABLE SLIDING JIG

P

A

A

A

A

G

G

G

G

1/8 x 1/2" SLOT (TYPICAL)

NO. 4 DRILL, 2" DEEP (2 PLACES)

A

4-3/4"

Q

2-3/4"

J

5/16"-DIA. HOLE (8 PLACES)

NO. 4 DRILL, 2" DEEP (2 PLACES)

2" SQUARES

G

G

2"

1/8"

1/8"

Z

1/2"

Y

1/4"

SOLDER PIVOT PIN TO SLIDE

12"

X

DETAIL PIECE X

B

ZZ

S

DRILL AND COUNTERSINK FOR NO. 12 SCREW (4 PLACES)

45°

5-1/2"

B

22-1/2°

11"

DETAIL PIECE B

5/32"-DIA. HOLE FOR 5/8" NO. 6 RH SCREW (6 REQD.)

3/64"-DIA. HOLE FOR 1/2" BRAD (6 REQD.)

ROUND OFF ENDS

M

2-1/4"

3/4"

1/2"

DETAIL PIECE M

Mini-maxi gateleg table

■ YOU CAN'T BEAT this table for versatility—use it in living or family room or out on the patio when entertaining a group. It'll comfortably seat up to 12 people—then fold away into 9 inches of space after the party.

GATELEG CONCEPT is centuries old—and still a good way to gain extra seating in a hurry when entertaining. This modern unit is easy to build.

V-GROOVES are made on panel edges with shaper. Feed in work from both ends to prevent splintering.

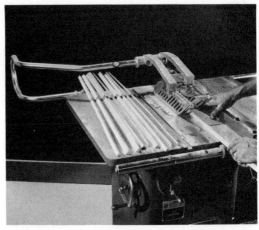

ANGLED INSERT STRIPS are ripped from solid lumber using hollow-ground planer blade, slow feed rate.

EXTREME CARE should be taken when you glue up gatelegs and framing to be sure assembly is square.

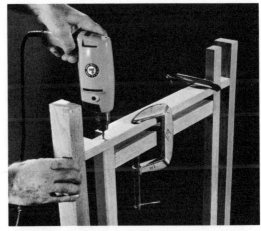

WHEN YOU BORE HOLES for pivot pins, clamp the gatelegs firmly to avoid any chance of movement.

ASSEMBLY is glued and screwed to divider strip. Slight edge-rabbet allows flush seating against hinge.

PIANO HINGE is positioned and screwholes marked so you can drill pivot holes before fastening hinges.

STRIPS are glued to two sides, then passed through shaper to obtain mitered corner on the strip ends.

COMPLETED GATELEG ASSEMBLY, ready to be installed, consists of pair of gatelegs, one leg frame.

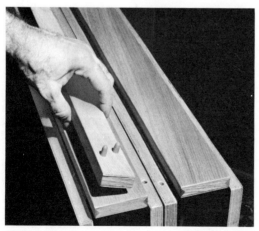

CENTER INSERT STRIP has two projecting pins to hold midsection in place when table is not expanded.

The table shown is of white oak veneer cabinet-grade plywood. This is a high-quality wood and, when finished properly, it will give your table the look of expensive furniture. If you are building yours for family room or patio use where it might be subject to greater abuse, you might consider using fir plywood (A-D) and covering the table entirely with a plastic laminate.

Since the four main tops are cut from two 4x8-ft. panels, lay out the sections so the grain runs parallel to the 36-in. dimension. This will avoid any chance of mismatched grain patterns butting end to end.

Connect each pair of tops to division strips with piano hinges. Recesses for the hinges need not be made on the bottom side of the panels. Instead, do the routing on the top of each frame cross member to take up the thickness of the hinge. Notice that the continuous hinges are spaced; this is essential to provide clearance for the swinging leg units.

Precision is a must

Construct the gate legs accurately. *If they are out of square full-face or edgewise, they won't operate properly*. If you don't own a drill press, disregard the blind dowel joints indicated in the drawings: instead, clamp the pieces together and bore dowel holes through from the outside with a portable drill. Dowel ends can be left exposed or driven in to allow room for wood plugs cut from the same lumber. Check for squareness after clamping and before the glue sets.

When the outer leg framing is complete, you can bore holes for the pivots. Securely clamp a leg section to the frame and bore ¼ x 1½-in. holes into both ends. Be sure to mark each subassembly so they don't get mixed up. Don't drive in the pins until all parts are sanded and finish-coated.

The pivots are cut from ¼-in. steel rod and one end is ground slightly rounded to facilitate driving. Fit should be snug so they'll stay in place, yet offer a slight resistance so the gatelegs don't swing loosely. Six No. 10 x 1¼-in. wood screws, and glue, secure the leg assembly to the dividing strip. When both sections are completed, butt them together and install a piano hinge to connect the inside table leaves.

Cut an insert strip to snug-fit the void. This filler strip fills the gap while a pair of projecting pins near each end serve to "lock" the two main sections together. The pins can be steel rod or slightly tapered dowels set firmly into the strip.

To expand the table, you simply remove the center strip and extend the desired leaves.

For a finish that brings out all the natural beauty of oak, mix together some raw sienna oil color and natural wood filler. Work the filler well into the open grain, then wipe clean with burlap. Allow to dry for 24 hours; then apply several coats of a clear, semigloss wood finish.

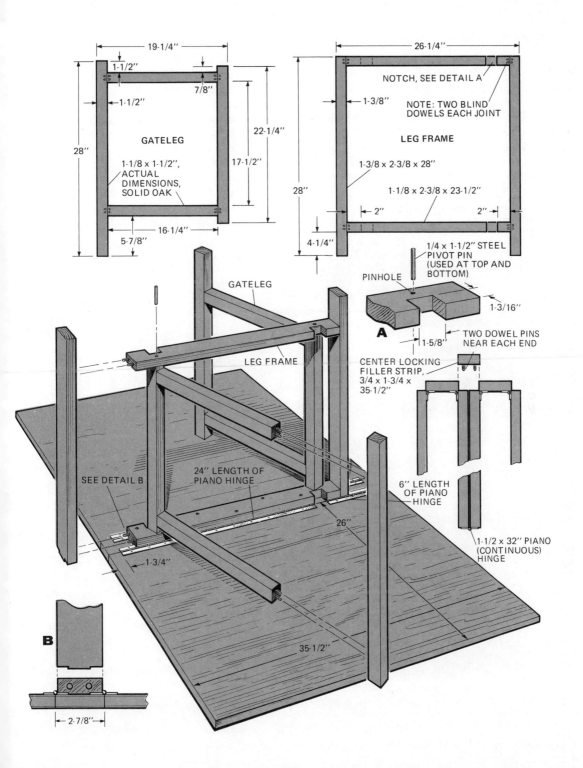

19-1/4"

1-1/2"

7/8"

1-1/2"

28"

22-1/4"

17-1/2"

GATELEG

1-1/8 x 1-1/2",
ACTUAL
DIMENSIONS,
SOLID OAK

16-1/4"

5-7/8"

26-1/4"

NOTCH, SEE DETAIL A

NOTE: TWO BLIND
DOWELS EACH JOINT

1-3/8"

LEG FRAME

1-3/8 x 2-3/8 x 28"

1-1/8 x 2-3/8 x 23-1/2"

28"

2"   2"

4-1/4"

1/4 x 1-1/2" STEEL
PIVOT PIN
(USED AT TOP AND
BOTTOM)

PINHOLE

1-3/16"

A

1-5/8"

TWO DOWEL PINS
NEAR EACH END

GATELEG

LEG FRAME

CENTER LOCKING
FILLER STRIP,
3/4 x 1-3/4 x
35-1/2"

SEE DETAIL B

24" LENGTH OF
PIANO HINGE

6" LENGTH
OF PIANO
HINGE

26"

1-3/4"

1-1/2 x 32" PIANO
(CONTINUOUS)
HINGE

B

35-1/2"

2-7/8"

Victorian sideboard

■ THIS OAK SIDEBOARD (often called a server) satisfies one of the biggest needs in a dining room—an attractive place to store infrequently used items such as bowls, vases and large serving platters.

The server was inspired by a number of similar pieces seen and studied at antique shows and auctions. Most of the originals were about 90 percent oak, with poplar used for the case back, drawers and sides. Some, of course, were constructed of mahogany.

To hold costs down, this sideboard was built with solid oak for all exposed members. You can economize by using ¾-in. plywood for interior partitions, carcass floor, the back and drawers. Purists, if they prefer, can use oak throughout, but such construction will drive up the cost considerably.

Selecting the marble top

Before you start building, make a trip to the nearest source of marble to discuss the various types of marble and their costs.

You can use a rich-looking, handsome Italian marble as shown; the ¾-in.-thick slab, which was cut specially to fit the cabinet, cost $150. The stonemason charged another $40 to deliver the slab. Costs will vary where you live.

Once you know the marble you want, and its cost, you can start building your cabinet. *Do not order the marble slab until you have finished building the cabinet.* Once the carcass is assem-

THIS ELEGANT SIDEBOARD (often called a server) is created in oak and topped with ¾-in.-thick Italian marble.

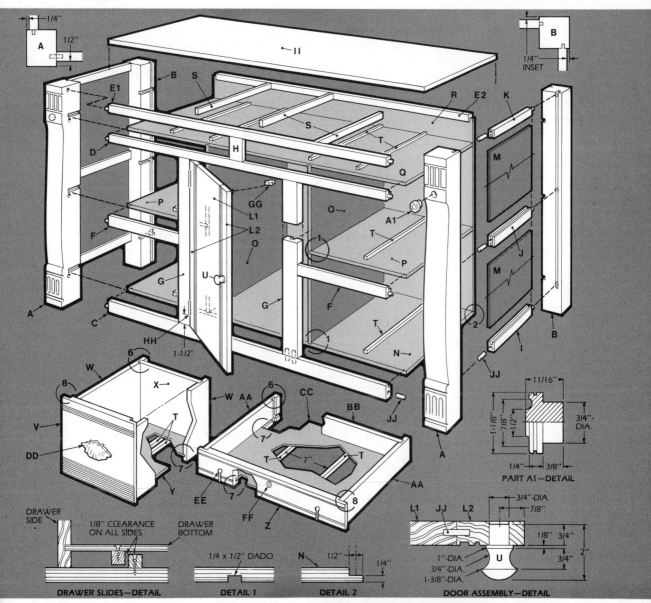

bled, you can measure the top and have the mason cut the slab to suit your piece exactly. Because of the chance of chipped corners, you don't want the marble to overhang the cabinet on any side. For the sake of appearance, you don't want the marble set back from the edges, either.

Building the cabinet

Start by laminating the stock for the four legs. Rip the boards slightly overwidth and join them, using glue and clamps. While these are drying, you can lay out and cut the rails for the end sections and front facing. Cut the parts slightly oversize at this stage and fit them neatly as you assemble each section.

The next day, carefully trim all four legs to the

CHANCES ARE you won't be able to buy 4x4 oak stock locally. Consequently, legs are made of glued-up 1-in. boards.

exact same size. Your best bet for avoiding a wobbly cabinet (caused by one leg being shorter than the others) is to first square one end on all four legs using the radial-arm saw. Then set up a stop block and trim all the second ends, one after the other. For each leg, tightly butt the first-cut end against the stop, and they will all be cut to identical length.

Using clamps and strips of wood, assemble a jig to hold the legs, one at a time, on your workbench. Using standard router procedures, set up the guides and stops for routing the vertical grooves at the top and bottom of each leg. Do the stopped grooves using a core box bit.

The front faces of both front legs are shaped. To get the contour shown in the drawing, make a

pattern on ¼-in. hardboard. When you're satisfied with the shape, transfer it to both front legs to serve as a guide for your shaping step.

Secure the first leg in your bench-top jig and start the shaping, using a sharp spoke shave, rasp, block plane and belt sander. Using the 3 x 21-in. belt sander with 80-grit paper helped speed up the task considerably. The shaping of the legs is the most time-consuming aspect of the entire project. So settle in and accept the fact that you will be doing it for a while.

Bore the holes at front to receive the decorative turned buttons. Turn the buttons on your lathe, using oak from the same stock used for the carcass. The button tenons should be cut for a neat—not loose—fit in their mating holes. Apply

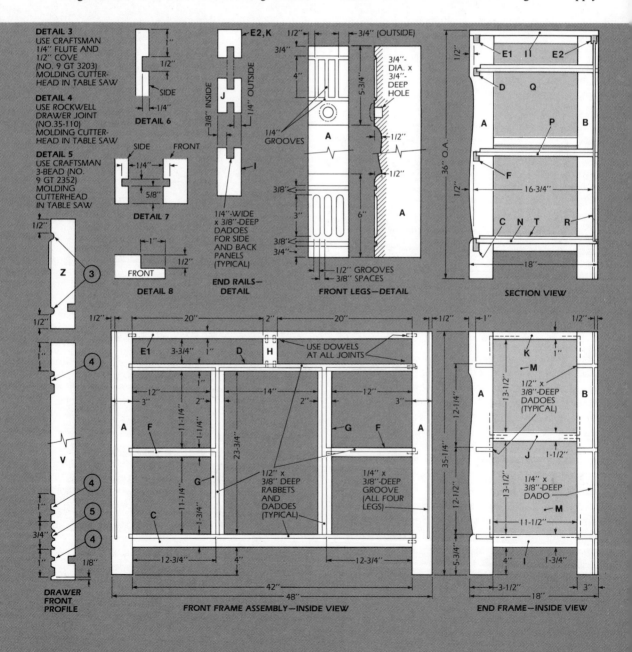

glue sparingly and insert button tenons into holes; lay legs on their back sides and put a weight on top of each button. Allow to dry overnight.

Make up the side (end) assemblies. Carefully lay out for the dadoes that will receive the drawer shelves. The latter do not butt tightly against the panels. Since the wells will be occupied by drawers, the shelves merely serve as a base for the drawers.

Assembling the cabinet

Assemble the cabinet as shown in the drawing. Dowels are used between rails and legs. And since the piece will be topped by a marble slab, there is no need to install a wood top. However, do install the front-to-back pieces (S). These are needed to support the marble.

Once the cabinet is assembled, you can take measurements and build the drawers and door. Mark a number in an inconspicuous spot in each well and use the numbers on drawer backs to ensure that each is returned to its proper position in the cabinet.

All hardware on the cabinet is purchased. You can buy the hinges locally, but for authenticity you can order the wooden and pendant pulls, knobs and key escutcheon plates from mail order houses.

Do as the professionals do and get most of your sanding out of the way before assembling the cabinet. The flat areas can be sanded to the 120-grit stage before assembly. The final touch-up, with 150-grit paper, can be done after the cabinet is built.

Dust off the piece and apply the stain of your choice. On the original, 4 parts Danish Walnut were mixed with 1 part contemporary mahogany. The stain should be applied to one area at a time and you should make every effort to keep the stain on each section for an identical length of time. Wipe off excess stain with a lint-free cloth and set aside to dry overnight.

Next day, smooth any raised "whiskers" using 180-grit paper with a light touch. Dust off and wipe with a tack cloth before applying the sealer.

The sealer coat used here is 3-lb. cut water-white shellac thinned 50 percent with denatured alcohol. Apply the shellac using a quality bristle brush. Allow the sealer to dry overnight.

The next day, sand lightly where needed using 180-grit paper. Dust off and wipe with a tack cloth. Pour off a small amount of the varnish (a half-full 1-lb. coffee can is just about right) and thin it 50 percent with turpentine. Apply the varnish, making sure you finish by tipping off.

MATERIALS LIST

VICTORIAN SIDEBOARD

Key	No.	Size and description (use)
		BASE CABINET
A	2	3 x 3½ x 35¼" oak (front leg)
A1	2	11/16 x 1⅛"-dia. (rosette)
B	2	3 x 3 x 35¼" oak (rear leg)
C	1	⅞ x 1¾ x 42" oak (bottom front rail)
D	1	⅞ x 1 x 42" oak (lower front rail)
E1	1	⅞ x 1 x 42" oak (upper front rail)
E2	1	⅞ x 1 x 42" oak (upper back rail)
F	2	⅞ x 1¼ x 12" oak (front rail)
G	2	⅞ x 2 x 23¾" oak (cabinet stile)
H	1	⅞ x 2 x 3¾" oak (stile)
I	2	⅞ x 1¾ x 11½" oak (end rail)
J	2	⅞ x 1½ x 11½" oak (end rail)
K	2	⅞ x 1 x 11½" oak (end rail)
L1	1	¾ x 8⅞ x 23⅝" oak (core panel)
L2	2	⅞ x 2½ x 23⅝" oak (door stile)
M	4	¼ x 12¼ x 14¼" oak plywood (end panels)
N	1	½ x 16⅞ x 42¾" A/C plywood (bottom)
O	2	½ x 16⅜ x 24¼" A/C plywood (vertical dividers)
P	2	½ x 13¼ x 16⅜" A/C plywood (shelf)
Q	1	½ x 16⅜ x 42¾" A/C plywood (top)
R	1	¼ x 28⅛ x 42¾" A/C plywood (back)
S	3	⅞ x 1 x 15½" oak (cleats)
T	20	½ x ½ x 15½" mapkle (drawer slides)
U	1	1⅜-dia. x 2" (wood knob)
		DEEP DRAWER (4 REQD.)
V	4	⅞ x 11⅛ x 11⅞" oak (front)
W	8	½ x 9⅜ x 16⅛" A/C plywood (sides)
X	4	½ x 10¼ x 11⅛" A/C plywood (back)
Y	4	¼ x 11⅛ x 16¼" A/C plywood (bottom)
		SHALLOW DRAWER (2 REQD.)
Z	**2**	**⅞ x 3⅝ x 19⅞"** oak (front)
AA	4	½ x 3½ x 16⅛" A/C plywood (sides)
BB	2	½ x 2⅝ x 18⅜" A/C plywood (back)
CC	2	¼ x 16¼ x 18¾" A/C plywood (bottom)
DD	4	Carved oak pull
EE	4	Pendant pulls
FF	2	False keyhole
GG	2	Double roller catch
HH	2	1½ x 2½" hinge
II	1	¾ x 18 x 48" Italian marble

Misc.: ⅜-in.-dia. dowels; 100-, 12-, 150- and 180-grit sandpaper, carpenter's glue, tack cloth.

Let the piece dry at least 24 hours. Next day, apply the finish coat of varnish as it comes from the can. Pour off the amount you think you will need. (It is never wise to use the large container as your work container. Neither should you pour back any varnish that has been exposed to the air.)

Use a varnish that gives a waxed, or hand-rubbed look to the piece. Let the piece cure for about a week before using it.

Dollhouse you can build

■ WELCOME TO the world of miniatures by way of our Victorian dollhouse.

The dollhouse might well become an heirloom in your family. Certainly any child of almost any age would be proud to own it.

The exterior is premade clapboard painted white. Shingles are made from chipboard strips. The sloping roof over the porch is made from three pieces of wood attached to a subroof.

Materials

To make the house, you'll need two 4x8 sheets of finished plywood, one ¼-in. thick and one ½-in. thick. You'll also need: 8 ft. of 1x2-in. pine strips for the exterior trim and porch trim; 8 strips of 22x⁵⁄₁₆-in. molding for the baseboards and livingroom ceiling trim; one strip ½-in. wide of decorative molding for the top of the pillars and porch; 16 windows; one door; white glue for gluing joints; rubber cement for gluing wallpaper; ¾-in. brads for nailing the exterior molding; finishing nails for attaching partitions to the ceilings; 1x8 flathead wood screws for joining the outer shell of the house; metal filigree trim for the rooftop (available at lamp stores); piano hinge 24-in. long (a 30-in. hinge is easily cut); two caster bearings for ease in opening the house front; three sheets 22x30-in. chipboard for shingles; paint; wallpaper; 18 sheets of 3½x22-in. clapboard siding; latch.

Steps for assembling

First cut the pieces out, making proper spaces for your windows and door. Use the layout diagram for the arrangement of parts, but follow the dimensions given for cutting.

Attach sides and back with screws in predrilled holes. Join the porch according to the exploded drawing and attach it to the house front. Construct the roof. Glue the roof trim and paint it black. Install painted windows and door. Paint and paper the interior.

Installing inner walls

The inner walls are installed a floor at a time. Glue first-floor walls to the floor. Insert the second floor and nail it to the first-floor walls. (You'll have to retouch the nail holes.) For additional strength, predrill from the exterior and screw the second floor to the house shell. Continue until all floors are installed. Then nail on the painted clapboard.

Furnishings and accessories

You can represent virtually every detail in life in miniature form. Many of the materials needed are right at hand. The standard scale when working with miniatures is one inch to the foot.

■ Books and magazines: Check book club ads for pictures of tiny books. Cut these out and paste them to a piece of wood. The rows of books in our Victorian house bookcase were drawn on strips cut from file folders, folded and glued to form a hollow rectangle.

■ Bookcases: The bookcase in our Victorian library was made from ⅛-in. beechwood joined with white glue and decorated with narrow molding.

■ Chandeliers: Crystal chandeliers can be made from tiny beads glued or wired together.

■ Curtains: The curtains for our houses were cut from material that doesn't ravel, gathered at the top and tied back with bits of yarn. You can glue them to the house.

■ Floor coverings: Magazine illustrations of carpet and parquet can be glued to the wood floor, then lightly varnished.

■ Food: Modeling clay painted with enamel and varnished makes delectable pastries, vegetables, fruit and breads. Or use bits of wax crayons to make fruit.

■ Stairs: Precut stringers of thin hardwood to which you can glue treads and risers are available.

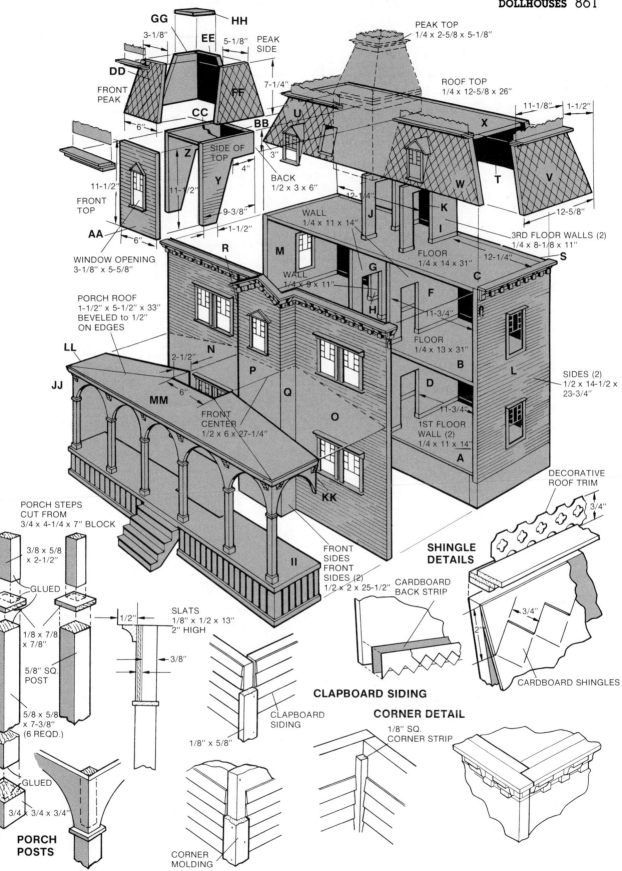

GG
HH
3-1/8"
EE
5-1/8"
PEAK SIDE
DD
FRONT PEAK
FE
7-1/4"
PEAK TOP
1/4 x 2-5/8 x 5-1/8"
CC
6"
ROOF TOP
1/4 x 12-5/8 x 26"
11-1/8"
1-1/2"
11-1/2"
FRONT TOP
AA
6"
WINDOW OPENING
3-1/8" x 5-5/8"
BB
U
X
Z
SIDE OF TOP
Y
11-1/2"
4"
3"
BACK
1/2 x 3 x 6"
9-3/8"
1-1/2"
12-1/4"
J
W
T
V
K
12-5/8"
3RD FLOOR WALLS (2)
1/4 x 8-1/8 x 11"
R
M
WALL
1/4 x 11 x 14"
I
FLOOR
1/4 x 14 x 31"
12-1/4"
S
C
PORCH ROOF
1-1/2" x 5-1/2" x 33"
BEVELED to 1/2"
ON EDGES
WALL
1/4 x 9 x 11"
G
F
H
11-3/4"
LL
N
2-1/2"
P
FLOOR
1/4 x 13 x 31"
B
JJ
MM
6"
FRONT CENTER
1/2 x 6 x 27-1/4"
Q
O
D
L
SIDES (2)
1/2 x 14-1/2 x
23-3/4"
KK
11-3/4"
1ST FLOOR WALL (2)
1/4 x 11 x 14"
A

PORCH STEPS
CUT FROM
3/4 4-1/4 x 7" BLOCK

3/8 x 5/8 x 2-1/2"

GLUED

1/8 x 7/8 x 7/8"

5/8 SQ. POST

5/8 x 5/8 x 7-3/8"
(6 REQD.)

GLUED

3/4 x 3/4 x 3/4"

PORCH POSTS

1/2"
3/8"

SLATS
1/8" x 1/2 13"
2" HIGH

FRONT SIDES
FRONT SIDES (2)
1/2 x 2 x 25-1/2"

II

CLAPBOARD SIDING
1/8" x 5/8"

CLAPBOARD SIDING

CORNER DETAIL
1/8" SQ. CORNER STRIP

CORNER MOLDING

SHINGLE DETAILS
CARDBOARD BACK STRIP
3/4"
3/4"
2"
CARDBOARD SHINGLES

DECORATIVE ROOF TRIM
3/4"

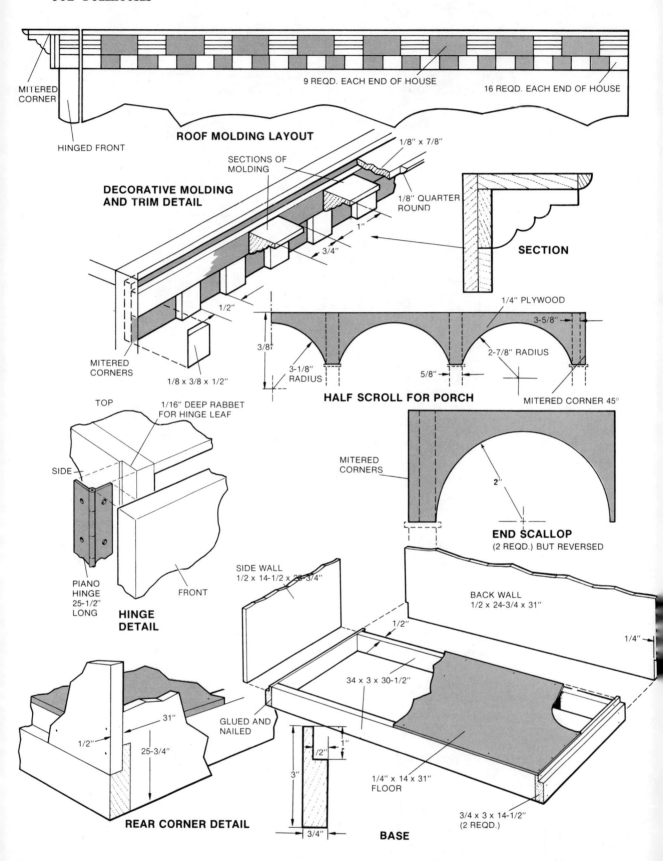

MITERED CORNER

HINGED FRONT

9 REQD. EACH END OF HOUSE

16 REQD. EACH END OF HOUSE

ROOF MOLDING LAYOUT

1/8" x 7/8"

SECTIONS OF MOLDING

DECORATIVE MOLDING AND TRIM DETAIL

1/8" QUARTER ROUND

1"

3/4"

SECTION

MITERED CORNERS

1/2"

1/8 x 3/8 x 1/2"

1/4" PLYWOOD

3-5/8"

3/8"

3-1/8" RADIUS

5/8"

2-7/8" RADIUS

HALF SCROLL FOR PORCH

MITERED CORNER 45°

TOP

1/16" DEEP RABBET FOR HINGE LEAF

SIDE

MITERED CORNERS

2"

PIANO HINGE 25-1/2" LONG

FRONT

HINGE DETAIL

END SCALLOP
(2 REQD.) BUT REVERSED

SIDE WALL
1/2 x 14-1/2 x 2⬚-3/4"

BACK WALL
1/2 x 24-3/4 x 31"

1/2"

1/4"

34 x 3 x 30-1/2"

GLUED AND NAILED

31"

1/2"

25-3/4"

1"

1/2"

3"

1/4" x 14 x 31"
FLOOR

3/4 x 3 x 14-1/2"
(2 REQD.)

REAR CORNER DETAIL

3/4"

BASE

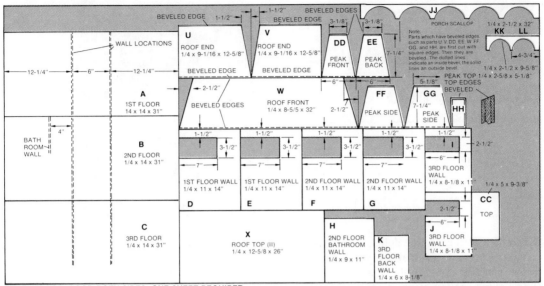

BEVELED EDGE
1-1/2"
BEVELED EDGE

1-1/2"
BEVELED EDGES
3-1/8" 3-1/8"
BEVELED EDGE

JJ
PORCH SCALLOP
1/4 x 2-1/2 x 32"

KK LL

WALL LOCATIONS

12-1/4" 6" 12-1/4"

U
ROOF END
1/4 x 9-1/16 x 12-5/8"
BEVELED EDGE

V
ROOF END
1/4 x 9-1/16 x 12-5/8"
BEVELED EDGE

DD
PEAK
FRONT

EE
PEAK
BACK

7-1/4"

Note.
Parts which have beveled edges,
such as parts U, V, DD, EE, W, FF,
GG, and HH, are first cut with
square edges. Then they are
beveled. The dotted lines
indicate an inside bevel, the solid
lines an outside bevel.

4-3/4"
1/4 x 2-1/2 x 9-5/8"

A
1ST FLOOR
14 x 14 x 31"

2-1/2"
BEVELED EDGES

W
ROOF FRONT
1/4 x 8-5/5 x 32"

6" 6"

FF
PEAK SIDE

2-1/2"

5-1/8"

GG
PEAK
SIDE

7-1/4"

PEAK TOP 1/4 x 2-5/8 x 5-1/8"
TOP EDGES
BEVELED

HH

BATH
ROOM
WALL

4"

B
2ND FLOOR
1/4 x 14 x 31"

1-1/2"
3-1/2"
7"
1ST FLOOR WALL
1/4 x 11 x 14"
D

1-1/2"
3-1/2"
7"
1ST FLOOR WALL
1/4 x 11 x 14"
E

1-1/2"
3-1/2"
7"
2ND FLOOR WALL
1/4 x 11 x 14"
F

1-1/2"
3-1/2"
7"
2ND FLOOR WALL
1/4 x 11 x 14"
G

1-1/2"
2-1/2"
6"
3RD FLOOR
WALL
1/4 x 8-1/8 x 11"
I

1/4 x 5 x 9-3/8"

CC
TOP

C
3RD FLOOR
1/4 x 14 x 31"

X
ROOF TOP (II)
1/4 x 12-5/8 x 26"

H
2ND FLOOR
BATHROOM
WALL
1/4 x 9 x 11"

K
3RD
FLOOR
BACK
WALL
1/4 x 6 x 8-1/8"

2-1/2"
6"
3RD FLOOR
WALL
1/4 x 8-1/8 x 11"
J

1/4" PLYWOOD, GOOD BOTH SIDES. ONE SHEET REQUIRED.

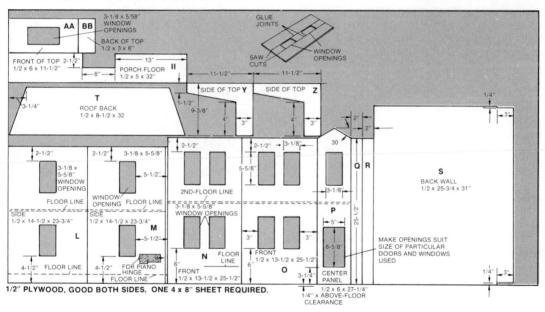

AA BB

3-1/8 x 5/58"
WINDOW
OPENINGS

BACK OF TOP
1/2 x 3 x 6"

FRONT OF TOP 2-1/2"
1/2 x 6 x 11-1/2"

6"

13"

PORCH FLOOR
1/2 x 5 x 32"

II

GLUE
JOINTS

WINDOW
OPENINGS

SAW
CUTS

11-1/2" 11-1/2"

SIDE OF TOP Y   SIDE OF TOP   Z

T
ROOF BACK
1/2 x 8-1/2 x 32

3-1/4"

1-1/2"
9-3/8"

4" 3"

4"

1/4"

3"

2"
2"

30

Q R

S
BACK WALL
1/2 x 25-3/4 x 31"

2-1/2"

3-1/8 x
5-5/8"
WINDOW
OPENING

FLOOR LINE

SIDE
1/2 x 14-1/2 x 23-3/4"

L

4-1/2" FLOOR LINE

2-1/2"
3-1/8 x 5-5/8"
WINDOW
OPENING

WINDOW
OPENING FLOOR LINE

SIDE
1/2 x 14-1/2 x 23-3/4"

M

4-1/2"
FOR PIANO
HINGE
FLOOR LINE

5-1/2"

5-1/2"

2-1/2"
2ND-FLOOR LINE

3-1/8 x 5-5/8"
WINDOW OPENINGS

N
FRONT
1/2 x 13-1/2 x 25-1/2"

FLOOR
LINE

6"

5-1/8"

3-1/8"

3"

3"
FRONT
O
1/2 x 13-1/2 x 25-1/2"

6"

3-1/4"

5"
6-5/8"

P

CENTER
PANEL
1/2 x 6 x 27-1/4"
1/4" x ABOVE-FLOOR
CLEARANCE

3-1/8"

25-1/2"

MAKE OPENINGS SUIT
SIZE OF PARTICULAR
DOORS AND WINDOWS
USED

1/4"

3"

1/2" PLYWOOD, GOOD BOTH SIDES, ONE 4 x 8" SHEET REQUIRED.

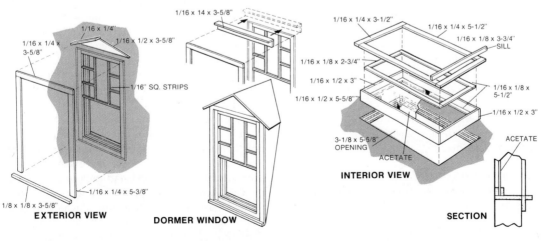

1/16 x 1/4 x
3-5/8"

1/16 x 1/4 x
3-5/8"

1/16 x 1/2 x 3-5/8"

1/16" SQ. STRIPS

1/8 x 1/8 x 3-5/8"

1/16 x 1/4 x 5-3/8"

EXTERIOR VIEW

1/16 x 14 x 3-5/8"

DORMER WINDOW

1/16 x 1/4 x 3-1/2"

1/16 x 1/4 x 5-1/2"

1/16 x 1/8 x 3-3/4"
SILL

1/16 x 1/8 x 2-3/4"

1/16 x 1/2 x 3"

1/16 x 1/2 x 5-5/8"

1/16 x 1/8 x
5-1/2"

1/16 x 1/2 x 3"

3-1/8 x 5-5/8"
OPENING

ACETATE

INTERIOR VIEW

ACETATE

SECTION

Dollhouse is a toybox, too

■ BUILD THIS charming dollhouse and you're certain to become the hero of your block. Its bright, cheerful design will blend well in any child's room; the two roomy floors and the spacious toy box are sure to make this a child's favorite toy. Your children will enjoy spending hours playing with it and then put all their toys away neatly when done. (Perhaps!)

Roof-panel safety feature

The hinged roof panel over the toy box is simply lifted for access to the storage space below. There is an important design note regarding the toy box roof that you should consider. We debated whether or not to install permanent hardware to hold the roof in the open position and decided against it, fearing that there is too great a chance of one child releasing the roof while another youngster is leaning into the box.

Similarly, if there is no hinge protection at all, there is a real risk of hinge damage caused by an exuberant child opening the rooftop too enthusiastically. We opted for a length of chain that prevents opening the roof beyond hinge capacity. *But be aware that the chain does not serve as a permanent stop in the open position.* You should instruct your child in the safe use of this roof/lid.

You'll need 1⅓ sheets of ½x48x96-in. fir plywood to build the house. Lay out the parts as shown in the cutting diagrams. Don't forget to allow for saw-kerf waste between the pieces. Since three roof panels require compound angle cuts, you should allow an extra inch or so for those parts to permit resawing after all square cuts have been made.

Obtaining straight cuts

Use a smooth-cutting plywood blade to cut out the parts. Work with a straightedge guide and portable circular saw or, if you can, use a table saw. If necessary, the cutting can be done with a sabre saw and straightedge.

Note that the pointed right-end panel (B) features two pointed fillers (R). You'll find it much simpler to do the cutting if you make straight through cuts along the parallel sides, then add ½x1 in. strips of solid pine to each edge of the top slants. Use glue and masking tape to hold them in place, then mark and cut the panel to the required angle.

Fill all voids and surface blemishes, usually on the C or D side, then sand all parts before assembly. If you mark all of the glue-joint lines and bore undersize pilot holes for the nails, you will ensure a neat, accurate assembly. This will also help prevent splitting of the plywood. Use carpenter's glue and 4d (1½ in.) finishing nails to join all pieces.

Order of assembly

The best order of assembly is as follows: Attach the back of the right end, then add the bottom of the storage compartment. Next, add the front (D), then the partition (F). The room ceiling and the floors go on next, followed by the left endpiece. Finally, add the triangular attic front.

The back roof panel (A) requires a 30° bevel cut along its top edge and a compound angle cut along the end abutting the house roof. To make this cut on the table saw, tilt the blade to 13° and set the miter gauge to 25°.

If desired, a beveled cleat (O on the back wall) can be nailed and glued in position on the inside of the roof panel to simplify and strengthen the assembly. This cleat *should not* extend beyond the attic area. Glue and nail the piece in place.

Cut both attic roof panels to size, beveled and mitered as shown. Once again, attach cleats (O).

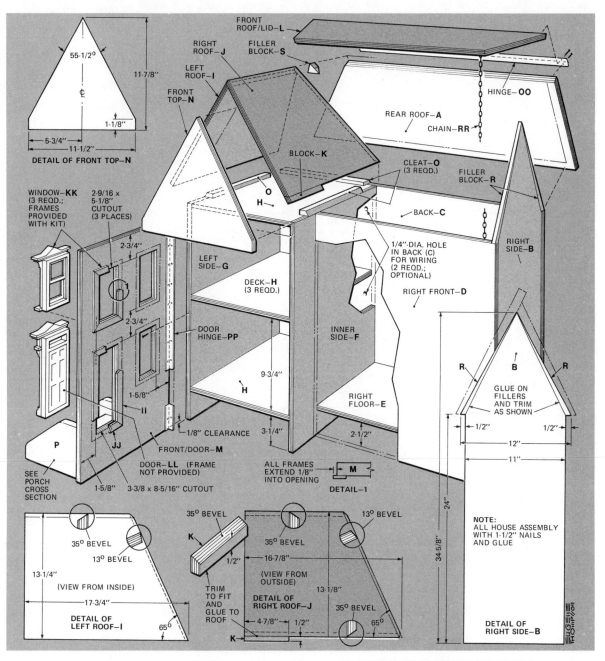

Note that the bottom edge of the right attic roof panel has a beveled setback. It's easier to achieve this notch by making a through bevel cut, then adding a short strip (K) to form the overhang. Also, when the panel is attached, it will project slightly above the peak. After the glue has dried, use a belt sander to true up the joint.

Mark and cut the lid/roof panel to fit and attach it with a 1¹/₁₆-in.-wide continuous hinge. Attach a length of chain and two screw eyes to limit the lid's travel.

MATERIALS LIST—DOLLHOUSE

Key	No.	Size and description (use) (All parts below are of ¹/₂″ plywood)
A	1	13³/₈ × 30¹/₂″ (roof, rear)
B	1	11 × 34⁵/₈″ (side, right)
C	1	24 × 29⁹/₁₆″ (back)
D	1	13¹/₁₆ × 24″ (front, right)
E	1	11 × 17⁹/₁₆″ (floor, right)
F	1	15 × 24″ (side, inner)
G	1	15 × 24″ (side, left)
H	3	10¹/₂ × 15″ (decks)
I	1	13¹/₄ × 17³/₄″ (roof, left)
J	1	13¹/₈ × 16⁷/₈″ (roof, right)
K	1	1 × 4⁷/₈″ (block, right roof; trim to size)
L	1	14¹/₈ × 24³/₈″ (roof/lid, front)
M	1	11¹/₂ × 22⁵/₈″ (front/door)
N	1	11¹/₂ × 11⁷/₈″ (front/top)

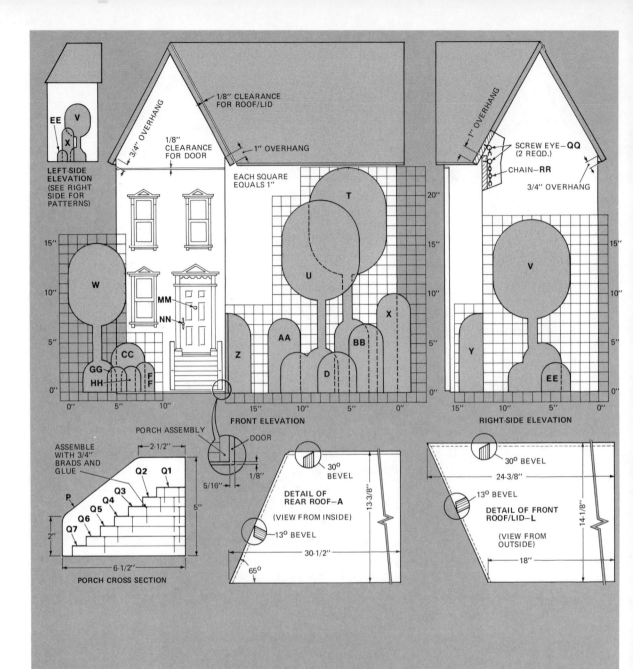

LEFT-SIDE ELEVATION
(SEE RIGHT SIDE FOR PATTERNS)

EE V X

3/4" OVERHANG

1/8" CLEARANCE FOR ROOF/LID

1/8" CLEARANCE FOR DOOR

1" OVERHANG

EACH SQUARE EQUALS 1"

W

CC
GG
HH
FF

MM
NN

Z AA D BB X

T U

FRONT ELEVATION

1" OVERHANG

SCREW EYE—QQ (2 REQD.)
CHAIN—RR
3/4" OVERHANG

V

Y EE

RIGHT-SIDE ELEVATION

PORCH ASSEMBLY
DOOR
5/16"
1/8"

ASSEMBLE WITH 3/4" BRADS AND GLUE

P
Q2 Q1
Q3
Q4
Q5
Q6
Q7

2-1/2"
5"
2"
6-1/2"

PORCH CROSS SECTION

30° BEVEL
13° BEVEL
65°

DETAIL OF REAR ROOF—A
(VIEW FROM INSIDE)

13-3/8"
30-1/2"

30° BEVEL
13° BEVEL

DETAIL OF FRONT ROOF/LID—L
(VIEW FROM OUTSIDE)

24-3/8"
14-1/8"
18"

Key	No.	Size and description (use)
O	3	1 × 10" (cleats; trim to fit)
P	2	5 × 6½" (porch side)
		(All parts below are of ½" pine)
Q-1	1	1½" × 4½" (porch step)
Q-2	1	2¼" × 4½" (porch step)
Q-3	1	3 × 4½" (porch step)
Q-4	1	3¾" × 4½" (porch step)
Q-5	1	4½ × 4½" (porch step)
Q-6	1	4½ × 5¼" (porch step)
Q-7	1	4½ × 6" (porch step)
R	2	1 × 15" (filler, right side; trim as shown)
S	1	2 × 2" (filler block; trim to fit)
		(All parts below are of ¼" plywood)
T	1	8 × 22"
U	1	8 × 18"

Key	No.	Size and description (use)
V	3	8 × 17"
W	1	5 × 16"
X	2	3½ × 10"
Y	1	2½ × 7½"
Z	1	2¼ × 7½"
AA	1	2¼ × 7"
BB	1	3⅞ × 7"
CC	1	3½ × 5"
DD	1	3¾ × 4"
EE	2	2¼ × 3"
FF	1	2 × 3"
GG	1	1¾ × 2½"
HH	1	2¼ × 2¼"
II	1	⅛ × ½ × 9¹/₁₆" pine
JJ	1	⅛ × ½ × 4⅛" pine
KK	3	Windows
LL	1	Door

Key	No.	Size and description (use)
MM	1	Door knocker
NN	1	Doorknob
OO	1	1⅙ × 24" roof hinge, continuous
PP	1	1⅙ × 22½" door hinge, continuous
QQ	2	Screw eyes
RR	1	25" chain

Misc: ¾" nails, 1½" nails, glue, pigmented shellac sealer, paint, sandpaper.

USE COMPOUND such as ZAR Wood Patch to fill voids before assembly.

START NAILS during dry assembly. Note that shoulders (O) on end panel have not yet been added.

BASIC BOX, ready for roof to be installed, as it's shown in drawings.

STRIP (K) is added to extend overhang after through bevel cut is made on bottom of roof panel.

BORE HOLES in corners, then use sabre saw to cut window openings.

MITERED FRAMING strips are installed for window and door backup. Frame is not supplied with door.

Handsome windows

The windows and door are store-bought ready-mades. We used Victorian-style units that are remarkably well detailed: The double-hung windows actually open and close, as does the door.

Lay out the openings for the windows and door, then bore a small blade-entry hole in each corner; use a sabre saw with a fine-tooth blade to make the cutouts.

The windows come with mitered frame members for use in trimming the back side. Rear frame strips are not supplied with the door, but can be easily made with 1/8x1/2-in. pine stock.

Build the stairway as a unit and attach it directly to the front panel of the house. Allow clearance at the bottom so it won't bind against a floor or table as it swings.

The stylized trees and shrubs are cut from 1/4x36x48-in. fir plywood.

Finishing the project

Apply a coat of primer sealer to all surfaces, but leave small, bare patches of wood where trees and shrubs will be glued. Don't paint the backs of the trees and shrubs.

Trees, windows and front door are attached with glue and 3/4-in. brads after *all* painting is done.

The dollhouse shown here was painted with latex interior semigloss enamel. To obtain vari-colored trees and shrubs, we poured some green paint into a separate container and darkened it with burnt umber pigment from a tube.

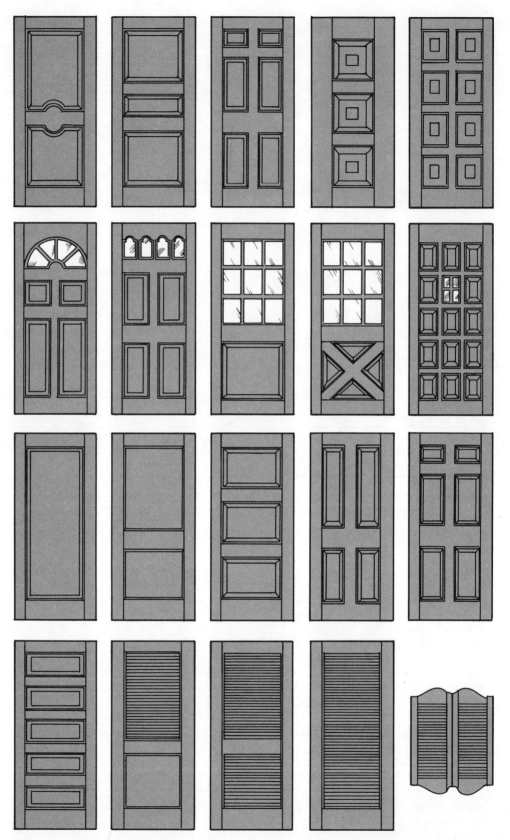

Standard doors include both flush and raised panel designs, shown here. Only a few of these styles are usually stocked by a retailer. Some glazed doors are available with an optional plastic grid to make a mullioned effect.

Doors

Exterior doors

Exterior doors come in three types: flush panel, panel, and glazed (with glass). There are two types of door cores: solid and hollow; solid core doors are generally used for exterior doors because they are stronger. Exterior doors also are available with steel and hardboard faces. Both types are difficult to tell from wooden doors when finished. Some brands are available prefinished.

Flush panel doors have wood, hardboard, or metal fastened to a frame and core of wood. As a rule, solid cores are made of blocks of wood laminated together, similar to a butcher block. The core may also be made of particleboard.

Panel doors—sometimes called raised panel doors—are made of styles and rails into which panels are fitted; the panels may be wood, glass or sometimes plastic.

Glazed doors include French doors and doors with multiple glass insert panels.

Sizes

Door sizes are stated in this way: 2/8 x 80; 3/0 x 78, 2/0 x 76. The first number is the width of the door in feet and inches; the second number is the length of the door in inches. In the example above, a 2/8 door is 2 feet, 8 inches wide, or 32 inches wide, by 80 inches long. A 3/0 door is 36 inches wide; a 2/0 door is 24 inches wide.

There are two ways to measure the wall opening for the door. If the opening is rough, that is, it hasn't been cased, allow 1½ inches at the top and side jambs and at the bottom for the casing and fitting in a typical installation. Be sure to check any door manufacturer's instructions; they may call for a special measurement. If the opening is finished, that is, it has been cased, measure from the inside jamb across to the opposite inside jamb and from the inside top header to the threshold. If you are replacing a door, simply measure the old door for the correct new door measurement.

Handedness

Exterior and interior doors are *handed,* that is, left- or right-handed. To identify a door's handedness, stand on the side of the door that opens *toward* you. If the door is hinged on the right side, it is a right-handed door and will be stamped RH. If the door is hinged on the left side, it is a left-handed door, stamped LH.

Standard door thicknesses are 1⅜ and 1¾ inches, although you can buy thicker and thinner doors. Locksets are sold by door thickness. Before you buy a lockset, be sure to measure the thickness of the door.

Interior doors

Interior doors in stock usually are limited to flush panel and raised panel doors with hollow core construction. The choice of styles includes single doors, single doors with a cutout for locksets, and pre-hung doors. Special types may be ordered; delivery usually is within several days.

Hollow cores are made up of a roughly two-inch framework of wood with strips of wood spaced throughout the length; the filler may also be cardboard or hollow wooden discs. Hollow core doors are usually reinforced with a wood block at the lockset location, providing a solid surface through which the lockset is attached to the door.

Pre-hung doors

Pre-hung doors are hung, or hinged, in a framework that includes the header, side jambs, and casings. One side of this framework dovetails into the other side. When the door is installed, the frame is separated and one side is fastened to the stud framing around the door opening. Then the other side of the frame is fastened on. The door is finished by installing a lockset; sometimes the lockset is installed on the door. Pre-hung doors in stock often are limited to flush panel styles. The panel usually is lauan wood (a type of mahogany), which can be sealed and left natural, stained, or enameled.

Hanging a door

■ IT TAKES CARPENTRY skill to hang a door so it swings properly—opening and closing as it should. But the average handyman, armed with knowledge, the right tools and a little common sense, can accomplish the job successfully. Here, we supply the know-how (architectural standards plus techniques). Now it's up to you to supply the common sense and muscle. Once you have hung a door correctly, you have acquired a valuable basic skill.

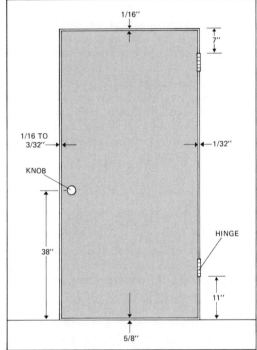

DOOR CLEARANCES and locations for door hardware are standard, as shown. If a third hinge is needed (exterior door), space it midway between top and bottom hinges. On exterior doors, allow clearance at bottom for threshold.

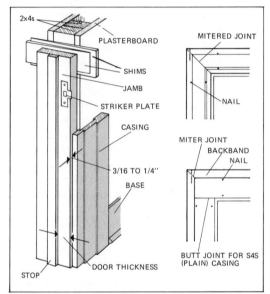

TO SET AN INTERIOR door frame (jamb), wedges or shingles are used between side jambs and the rough opening. When jambs are set flush and plumb, the wedges are driven tightly and jambs are nailed to studs with 8d finishing nails through the shingles. Casings are nailed to the framing studs and the jamb with 8d and 6d nails, respectively. Two types of casings are shown. Use mitered corners on shaped type, 4d finishing nails to hold miters closed tightly.

THERE ARE TWO TYPES of interior doors—panel and flush. Thickness is 1⅜ in. (exterior doors, 1¾ in.) and they come in varying widths and heights. Flush doors have plywood facings, light-weight cores; panel doors have solid stiles and rails with plywood panel inserts.

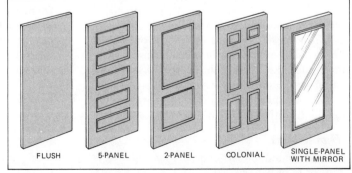

Trim sticking doors

WOODEN BOX

C-CLAMP

■ EVER HAD a door bind so it wouldn't close, or it wouldn't swing over a thick, new carpet? Few homeowners haven't had these problems with doors—particularly binding, for most wood doors swell periodically. Sometimes they expand so much they never shrink back to their former size. When that happens, you have no recourse but to remove the door and plane it. Or you must trim it with a saw if it's binding on a carpet. Not all doors bind because of moisture. Sometimes one won't operate properly because the screws have worked loose in a hinge, allowing the door to droop enough so that it won't open and close the way it should.

WHEN A DOOR MUST BE PLANED

When a door continues to stick even during dry weather and is hard to open, the only way to fix it is to plane it. Planing is done along the hinge edge of the door since you can't disturb the lock. Take down the door, remove its hinges and support it on edge. A wooden box is a good thing to clamp it to. If you must plane top and bottom, work from edge to center so you won't chip the corners.

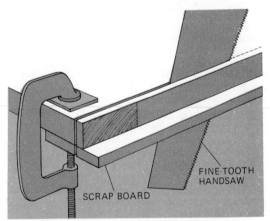

FINE-TOOTH HANDSAW

SCRAP BOARD

WHEN YOU HAVE TO SHORTEN A DOOR

When a new carpet is thicker than the old and a door drags on it, watch that you don't chip one side when you cut the door. Determine the amount you must take off, and draw a line across the door. Take the door down by knocking out the hinge pins, support it on a couple of padded sawhorses or boxes and clamp a scrap board to the underside of the door. The board not only prevents chipping the thin plywood facing on interior doors but helps keep the saw from running off the line when sawing as little as ¼ in. Use a fine-tooth saw.

WHEN A DOOR NEEDS SEALING

Doors usually swell during prolonged periods of rain, ice and snow. When the top and bottom edges of a door are not sealed, excessive moisture can enter the open end grain and cause the wood to expand and the door to widen. Common shellac is good for sealing the wood against moisture and it dries quickly, but you should wait for a dry spell; you don't want to seal the edges and trap any moisture that may be in the door at the time. Of course, to coat the bottom edge you must take the door down.

Shellac

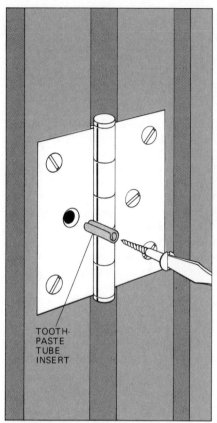

TOOTH-
PASTE
TUBE
INSERT

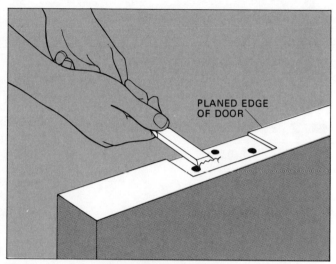

PLANED EDGE
OF DOOR

WHEN YOU HAVE TO PLANE OFF A LOT

When you have to plane off more than a little to relieve a binding door, you have to chisel the hinge pockets deeper to compensate for the amount you take off. Try to pare them an even amount. A properly set hinge leaf should be slightly deeper than flush. When the door has been planed enough to close properly, repaint the planed edge.

WHEN HINGES WORK LOOSE

Like anything that is used a great deal, a door that is opened and closed frequently puts a strain on the hinges that can eventually cause the door to bind. Usually you will find that a screw or two has worked loose, even to the point where it will no longer hold. When the trouble is found to be an enlarged hole, this hole must be shimmed. Sometimes a wooden matchstick and a little glue will do the trick, but an even better shim is one that's rolled from the soft metal of a toothpaste tube. Like a lead anchor, it will let the screw threads cut into the shim and spread it to fill the hole. Regular plastic screw plugs also can be used to shim an enlarged hole. In this case, the screw makes the plug expand and anchor itself tightly in the hole.

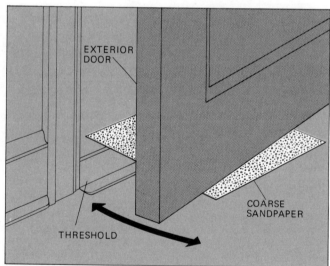

EXTERIOR
DOOR

COARSE
SANDPAPER

THRESHOLD

WHEN A DOOR DRAGS ON ITS THRESHOLD

If you can sand the bottom of a heavy exterior door that rubs on the threshold without removing it from its hinges, it's worth a try. A stunt that often does the trick is to work a sheet of coarse garnet paper under the door as shown above and then move the door back and forth. Little by little it will sand enough off to relieve the rubbing. When the dragging is beyond the sandpaper trick, you'll have to plane it.

Aluminum storm and screen repair

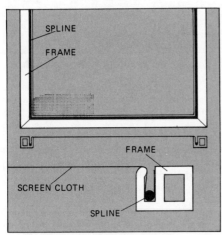

1. Typical aluminum screen

The screen cloth is secured by a plastic spline in frame groove. Replacing a torn window screen is simple if proper technique and tools are used. Begin by locating the ends of the spline in groove, lift them with an awl or screwdriver blade and pull the spline out of groove on all four sides of the frame. If the spline breaks, it must be replaced. In that event, save a sample of the old spline in order to purchase the correct replacement.

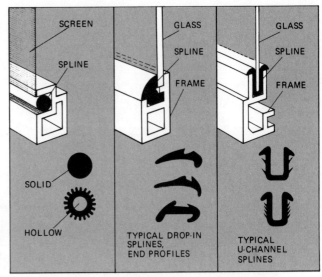

2. Splines for aluminum storms and screens

Splines are made in a variety of shapes. At left above are round splines, solid or hollow, used to secure screens to frames. There are two kinds of storm-sash frame, each with its own type of spline. Drop-in type, center, is easier to handle as it does not require disassembly of frame for re-glazing. Take-apart type, right, using U-channel splines, must be disassembled. Frame and spline designs vary considerably, depending upon the maker, but correct spline shape and size is available by the package or the roll

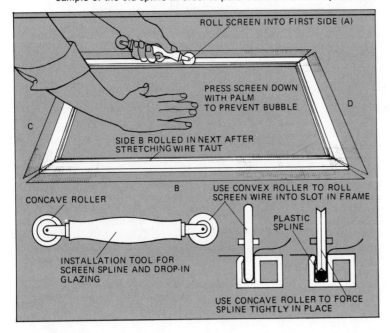

3. Reinstalling screen wire

Push old screen out from the back of frame. Measure outside length and width of frame and cut new screen at least 2 in. over-size in all directions. Holding screen down on frame, use installation tool's convex roller to force into groove with five or six passes—don't try it with one pass or screen will rip. Place spline on groove, force it in place with concave roller. Turn frame, repeat on opposite side, pulling screen tight and working convex roller down and to outside of frame. If frame bows, start over with new screen. If not, place spline with concave roller. Screen should now feel tight. Using scissors, make V-cuts in screen at corners to relieve tension; then finish the last two sides in the same way

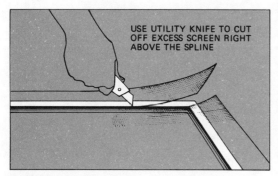

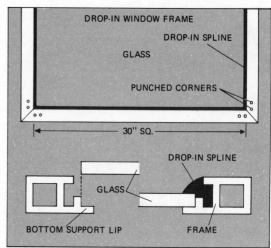

4. Trimming the wire

After screen has been grooved and locked in with spline on all four sides, insert tip of a utility knife just above spline in groove's outer side. Hold frame and run knife along inside edge. Excess screen can now be pulled away and discarded. Take care when cutting to avoid splines

5. Reglazing aluminum storm sash

Replacement of glass in aluminum storm sash requires precaution of wearing gloves and safety goggles. To remove glued-in glass, brush the pieces with paint remover; save a scrap piece to assure you buy the right thickness for your replacement pane. Frame above, a drop-in type, does not come apart. Measure inside dimensions including support lips. Cut window glass to size and carefully lay it inside the frame so that it rests on the lips. Insert drop-in spline by laying it on the window beveled side up and pushing it into the frame with your fingers. Repeat the procedure for the other three sides and the window is finished. Here, too, if the old spline breaks, replace it with a new one

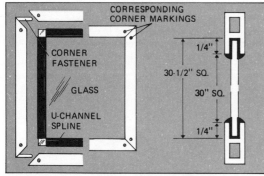

6. Assuring accurate reassembly

Take-apart frame, above, should be matched at three corners to assure accurate reassembly. For width and height of frame for glass, take distances between opposite U-channel bottoms. Be sure to allow (subtract) for spline. Fit U-channel spline over all four edges of the pane. Then using a wood or plastic mallet, gently tap on a section of the frame—one without corner fasteners—into place over the spline on the glass edge. Repeat on opposite edge, then line up frame sections to which corner fasteners are attached with corresponding holes on first two sides. After gently tapping frame together, replace corner screws or the clips as is seen at the sketch on the right

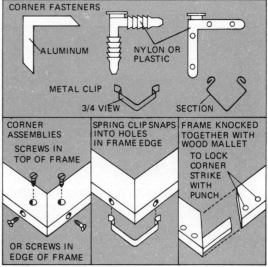

7. For smooth operation

Keep window tracks clean and spray with silicone lubricant. A mild cleaner and water will remove discoloration; avoid using abrasives

Stretch screen wire

Play it smart; let frame do stretching

Ripping the old wire from wooden frames and stapling on the new is simple enough—it's the stretching that's the tricky part. Trying to get it smooth and taut by hand not only is hard on the fingers but invariably results in a belly in the wire, no matter how you tug and pull.

Actually, it's not that hard a job. If you play it smart, the frame itself can be used to do the stretching. Bowing the frame slightly is the most common method. This can be done with a couple of jack sticks, as at right, or with blocks and C-clamps, as shown below. After the wire is stapled to each end and the bow relieved, the frame will straighten out and stretch the wire as taut as a drumhead. The stapling is completed along each side while the frame is flat. This method works best on full-length frames, with the frame supported on a couple of sawhorses or wooden boxes. It doesn't take much of a bow; in fact, you should avoid bowing the frame too much as this could result in the wire pulling out the staples or tearing loose.

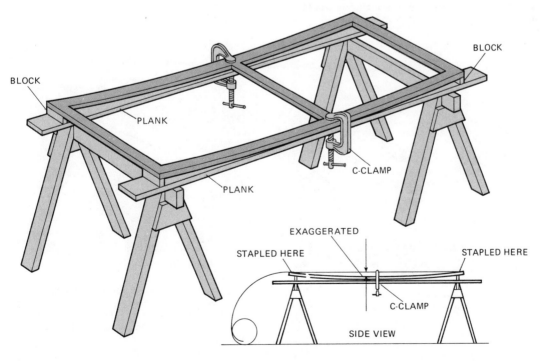

BLOCK

BLOCK

PLANK

PLANK

C-CLAMP

EXAGGERATED

STAPLED HERE

STAPLED HERE

C-CLAMP

SIDE VIEW

SCREEN WIRE is available in standard widths of 24, 26, 28, 30, 32, 36 and 42 inches. You have a choice of galvanized, aluminum, copper and fiberglass wire, and you may use either tacks or double-pointed screen staples to fasten it.

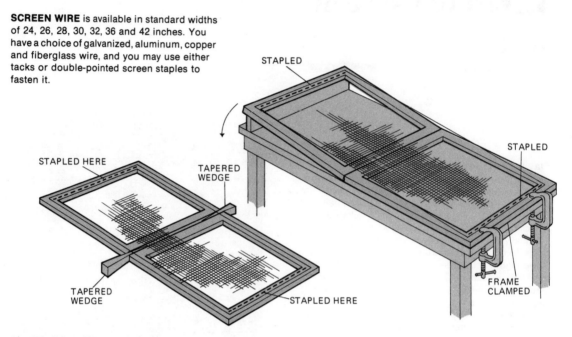

Small frames stretch each other

Small screens can be used to stretch the wire by covering two at a time (above). Frames are flat on a floor or table with one elevated a bit. In each case, they are butted and the wire stapled to the outer ends only. In method A, the wire is stretched by removing the block; in method B, it's done by forcing the frames apart with tapered wedges. Shown below is still another way for stretching wire on a full-length frame.

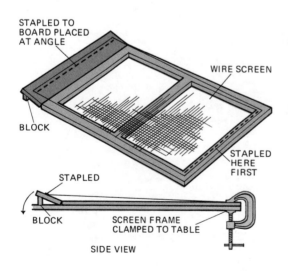

SIDE VIEW

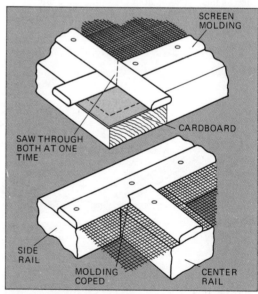

Slick molding trick

If you don't own a miterbox, you can do without one when mitering screen molding. Simply let one strip lap the other (above), then saw through both strips at a 45° angle at one time. Cardboard will protect frame from saw marks. Center-rail molding is coped to mate with side moldings.

Sliding glass doors let the outdoors in

■ THE PROBLEM FOCUSED on an attractive weekend retreat at the eastern tip of Long Island. This summer home and vacation hideout was its owner's delight, but it didn't give the indoors much of the outdoor beauty so precious to refugees from New York's urban pressures.

The good-looking results, from both inside and out, are obvious. The front porch has been transformed from a simple walkway leading to the front door to a small patio for lounging. The sliding glass doors not only give a great view of the countryside but brighten up the kitchen-dining area by letting in more sunlight. The increased exposure also gives better air circulation.

The important point, when laying out a job such as this, is to insure that the installation matches the architecture of the home. The job is not difficult. As shown in the existing and new

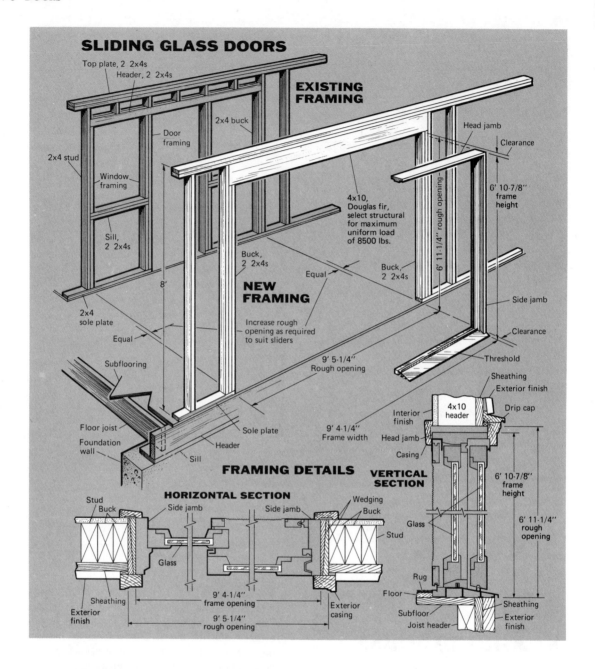

SLIDING GLASS DOORS

Top plate, 2 2x4s
Header, 2 2x4s

EXISTING FRAMING

2x4 buck

Door framing

Head jamb

Clearance

2x4 stud

Window framing

6' 10-7/8" frame height

4x10, Douglas fir, select structural for maximum uniform load of 8500 lbs.

Sill, 2 2x4s

6' 11-1/4" rough opening

8'

Buck, 2 2x4s

Equal

Buck, 2 2x4s

NEW FRAMING

2x4 sole plate

Increase rough opening as required to suit sliders

Side jamb

Equal

Clearance

Subflooring

9' 5-1/4" Rough opening

Threshold

Sheathing

Exterior finish

Drip cap

9' 4-1/4" Frame width

4x10 header

Floor joist

Interior finish

Foundation wall

Head jamb

6' 10-7/8" frame height

Sole plate

Casing

Header

Glass

6' 11-1/4" rough opening

Sill

FRAMING DETAILS

VERTICAL SECTION

HORIZONTAL SECTION

Stud
Buck

Side jamb

Side jamb

Wedging
Buck

Rug

Glass

Stud

Floor

Glass

9' 4-1/4" frame opening

Sheathing

Exterior casing

Subfloor

Sheathing

Exterior finish

9' 5-1/4" rough opening

Joist header

Exterior finish

structural drawings above, it consists basically of opening the wall and installing studs and header to suit the doors you buy. It pays to make an accurate scale drawing of the existing structure before you start. Then decide how big the sliding doors are that you wish to add. By laying out the new framing on tracing paper placed over the existing framing you will have an accurate picture of the raw materials you need.

Be sure the framing you install meets the minimum requirements of the Federal Housing Administration. If the area you intend to glass-in is longer than that shown here, be sure to check with the building department in your area to make certain that structural members meet the local code requirements.

When you are certain you have all the dimensions and materials correct, start by removing the existing framing. The new framing is constructed of 2 x 4s with the bucks on the end being doubled 2 x 4s for added strength. The top of the new framing is a 4 x 10 piece of Douglas fir. With the new framing in place, the door jamb is fitted into the opening and anchored securely.

Traverse rod installation

■ PUTTING UP new drapery rods so they stay is a job all homeowners face at times, whether they're moving into a new home or switching over to today's bold, new drapery hardware. Since the popular trend is to stack the draperies back off the glass, you won't always find a stud where you want it. If you do, you're lucky, but chances are you'll be faced with attaching the brackets to a hollow part of the wall. You can't drive plain screws into the plaster; they won't hold. The answer is a Molly fastener which is designed to hold anything securely to a wall without a stud.

Plan to place brackets for the rods above the casing, or at least 4 in. above the glass and an equal distance from the ceiling.

GLASS WIDTH	STACKBACK SPACE	ROD WIDTH
20″	20″	40″
26″	22″	48″
32″	24″	56″
38″	26″	64″
44″	28″	72″
50″	30″	80″
56″	32″	88″
62″	34″	96″
68″	36″	104″
75″	37″	112″
81″	39″	120″
87″	41″	128″
94″	42″	136″
100″	44″	144″
106″	46″	152″
112″	48″	160″
119″	49″	168″

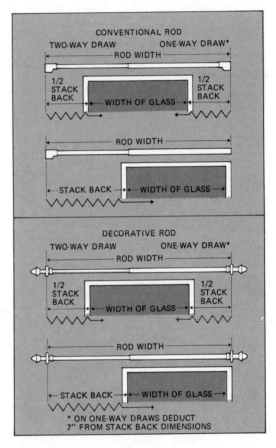

How to find the right rod length

With a draw treatment, it's best to have the draperies stack back over the window frame and wall, uncovering all the glass. To do this you must know the amount of wall space needed for the open panels before buying and installing the traverse rods. Use the chart at the left to find the correct rod length. Begin by measuring the glass width of your window. Say it's 38 inches wide. The chart shows you'll need 26 in. of wall for stack-back. So you add 38 and 26 in. and you'll see that you need a rod 64 in. long. The drawings above illustrate where the stack-back will be located. Stack-back is the amount of space occupied by open draw draperies. Space will vary depending on panel width, pleat spacing and fabric bulk. Since windows have two sides, you divide the stack-back distance in half (in this case 13 in.) to see how far the rod should extend beyond the glass. If you use one-way draperies, add the full 26 in. to one side

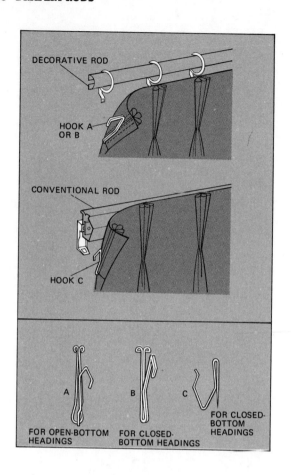

Selecting proper drapery hooks

The right drapery hooks can mean the difference between tip-tilt headings and those that stand properly erect. Always important, your choice of hooks is vital to the proper appearance of draperies hung on decorative traverse rods. At each window you will need one hook for each drapery pleat, plus four for returns and overlaps. On a decorative rod, the heading covers the pendants and falls just below the bottom of the rings. On a conventional rod, the heading extends to cover the rod. Thus hooks for conventional rods must be longer from the top of the hook to the top of the shank than hooks used for decorative rods

Ways to anchor brackets securely

Correct fastening devices are a must for proper installation of drapery hardware. Wood screws 1¼ in. long threaded the full length of the shanks are suitable for attaching brackets to studs. If wood studs can't be located or bracket-location falls between studs, Mollies (hollow-wall anchors) should be used as shown below. They are inserted in holes drilled through plaster or dry wall, tapped flush with the surface to embed the points and finally pulled up tight on the back by turning the screw that comes with the anchor. When mounting the modern, lightweight drapery rods on the wall, you can use plastic screw anchors. These easy-to-use tapered sleeve-type plugs are tapped in place in undersize holes drilled right through the plaster. Then simply find a full-thread wood screw of the proper size and turn it into the plug. As you turn it in, it spreads the split plastic sleeve and anchors it securely in place

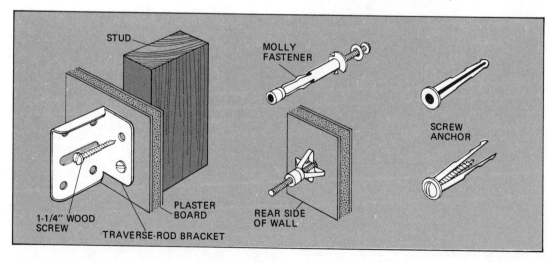

Drawer construction

■ THOUGH MANY do-it-yourselfers mistakenly think that making a drawer is beyond their abilities, no great mystery surrounds the task. The two keys to good drawer-making—whether using sophisticated joinery techniques or constructing the simplest drawer—are: 1. accurate measurements, and 2. perfectly square cuts.

Whether you are building a drawer from a working drawing or taking dimensions from a cabinet, study the drawing or cabinet carefully to determine the exact height, width and depth. Use the same kind of wood for drawer front as was used on the cabinet; drawer sides and back can be of less expensive nonwarped clear pine. The drawings on these pages give all the basics of good drawer construction. Study them carefully. Additional drawer know-how is spelled out in accompanying captions.

THREE MOST COMMON DRAWER FRONTS

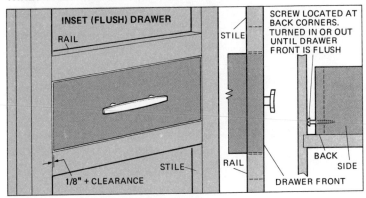

AN INSET flush drawer should have uniform clearance around the opening on all four sides. The usual clearance is ⅛ in. When laying out the drawer, carefully determine the length of the sides so that the drawer front will be perfectly flush with the stiles and rails. A pair of screws in the back corners will aid in aligning the drawer front if drawer is too short.

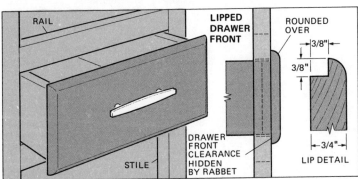

ROUNDED OR LIPPED fronts are most commonly used on kitchen cabinets. The advantage of this type front is that the lip conceals the gap between drawer and opening—thus, the ⅛-in. clearance mentioned above is not as critical. The lip is created by a ⅜-in.-sq. rabbet around the inside edges of the drawer front. This rabbet can be made with a router in one pass, or on a table saw in two passes. The remaining edge is usually rounded off with either a shaper or a block plane and belt sander. If you prefer a contemporary look, omit the rounding off step. A lipped drawer front can also be created by fastening ⅜-in. quarter-round moldings to the outside of each of the drawer edges.

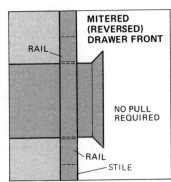

MITERING ON THE inside edge of a drawer front calls for careful cutting. After setting the table-saw blade to the desired angle, adjust the rip fence to leave a feather edge as shown. Cut ends of the front first (across the end grain), then make cuts with the grain. For safety, attach a wood face to your rip fence,

TYPICAL DRAWER JOINERY

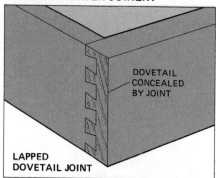

DOVETAIL CONCEALED BY JOINT

LAPPED DOVETAIL JOINT

THE DOVETAIL JOINT is the strongest you can use in drawer-making. A well-made dovetail joint will, literally, hold without glue—a fact old world craftsmen prided themselves on. Today the joint is made using a router equipped with a dovetail bit, and a dovetail template; instructions for use are packed with the template. Once you are familiar with the template, the joints are rather easy to make; to be safe, first perfect your technique on scrap wood.

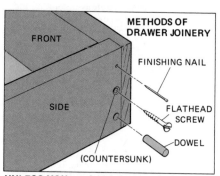

METHODS OF DRAWER JOINERY

FRONT

SIDE

FINISHING NAIL

FLATHEAD SCREW

DOWEL

(COUNTERSUNK)

UNLESS YOU are faithfully reproducing a period piece with nonglued dovetail joints, the chances are you will assemble your drawers using one of the three fastening methods shown. Regardless of which fastener you use, glue should be liberally applied to mating surfaces of pieces to be joined. For maximum strength, fasteners should be installed parallel to the drawer front. Thus, pull on a drawer creates a shear action on a fastener. This gives greater resistance to pull-out than if fasteners are installed perpendicular to front.

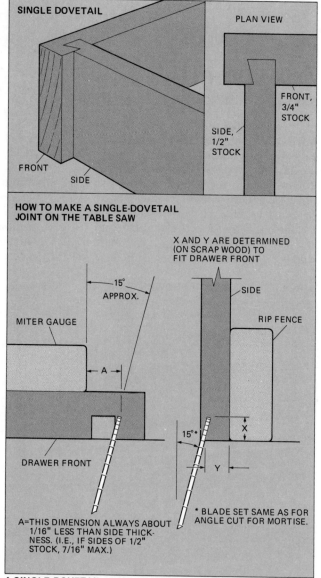

SINGLE DOVETAIL

PLAN VIEW

FRONT, 3/4" STOCK

SIDE, 1/2" STOCK

FRONT

SIDE

HOW TO MAKE A SINGLE-DOVETAIL JOINT ON THE TABLE SAW

X AND Y ARE DETERMINED (ON SCRAP WOOD) TO FIT DRAWER FRONT

SIDE

RIP FENCE

15° APPROX.

MITER GAUGE

A

DRAWER FRONT

15°*

X

Y

A=THIS DIMENSION ALWAYS ABOUT 1/16" LESS THAN SIDE THICKNESS. (I.E., IF SIDES OF 1/2" STOCK, 7/16" MAX.)

* BLADE SET SAME AS FOR ANGLE CUT FOR MORTISE.

A SINGLE-DOVETAIL can be cut on the table saw, but requires much care and laying out prior to cutting. Make test cuts on scrap lumber of exactly the same size and dimensions as will be used in drawer construction. Try all test cuts and fits before putting the blade to the project materials. First cut the dado about one-half the depth of the front. Then set the saw blade to about 15° and make the cut shown above left. Without disturbing the blade setting, make the mating angle cuts on the drawer sides. The blade can then be set at 0° and the triangular pieces cut out of the sides. Note: X and Y are determined on scrap wood first.

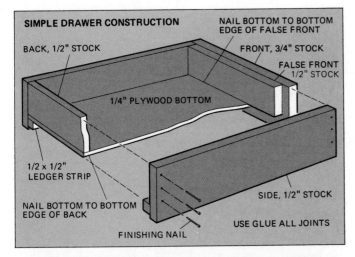

SIMPLE DRAWER CONSTRUCTION

NAIL BOTTOM TO BOTTOM EDGE OF FALSE FRONT

BACK, 1/2" STOCK

FRONT, 3/4" STOCK

FALSE FRONT 1/2" STOCK

1/4" PLYWOOD BOTTOM

1/2 x 1/2" LEDGER STRIP

NAIL BOTTOM TO BOTTOM EDGE OF BACK

FINISHING NAIL

SIDE, 1/2" STOCK

USE GLUE ALL JOINTS

THE DRAWER at left can be entirely constructed using hand tools only. After determining drawer-front dimensions, subtract thickness of sides and bottom. Assemble false front to front with glue and brads. Then cut the sides, back and bottom. Use ½ x ½-in. strips to make the ledger strips upon which the bottom rests. These are placed so top surface of bottom will be snug against bottom of false front and back. To assemble the drawer, apply glue, and nail sides to front as shown. With drawer on workbench, apply glue and install the back. Next, flop drawer, position the bottom on drawer frame and secure it with one nail. Before driving a second nail, check the drawer assembly with a square. Holding the drawer square, drive two more nails through bottom into back and false front. To finish assembly, using glue and brads, install the ledger strips beneath bottom on both sides. Recheck with square. Let dry.

A COMBINATION rabbet-and-fastener assembly provides a strong drawer. Here, you simply edge rabbet the drawer front to half the depth of the front and to a width equal to thickness of drawer sides. Test-fit the drawer dry (using brads). When you're satisfied with outside dimensions and squareness, the drawer can be permanently assembled using glue and fasteners.

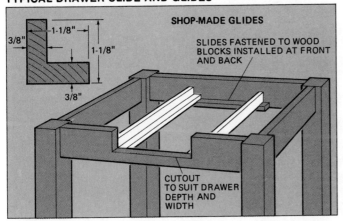

RABBETED DRAWER

BACK IS ATOP BOTTOM. BOTTOM IS NAILED TO BACK

BACK LET INTO HALF-DEPTH DADOES IN SIDES

FRONT

FINISHING NAIL

BOTTOM

BOTTOM "FLOATS" IN GROOVES IN SIDES AND FRONT

EDGE RABBET, HALF DEPTH OF FRONT

TYPICAL DRAWER SLIDE AND GLIDES

SHOP-MADE GLIDES

3/8"

1-1/8"

1-1/8"

3/8"

SLIDES FASTENED TO WOOD BLOCKS INSTALLED AT FRONT AND BACK

CUTOUT TO SUIT DRAWER DEPTH AND WIDTH

SHOP-MADE wood slides should be cut from ⁵/₄ x ⁵/₄ (1 ⅛ x 1 ⅛-in.) solid oak or other hardwood. Slides are fastened to blocks at front and back of cabinet. These blocks must be carefully set to assure that the drawer front is parallel to the cabinet front. For ease of operation, spray the slides at regular intervals with silicone.

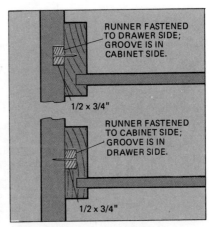

RUNNER FASTENED TO DRAWER SIDE; GROOVE IS IN CABINET SIDE.

1/2 x 3/4"

RUNNER FASTENED TO CABINET SIDE; GROOVE IS IN DRAWER SIDE.

1/2 x 3/4"

FAST METHOD of making slides is to groove either drawer sides or cabinet and attach hardwood guides to the mating member. To keep the cabinet sides from binding, it is a must that they be straight and unwarped.

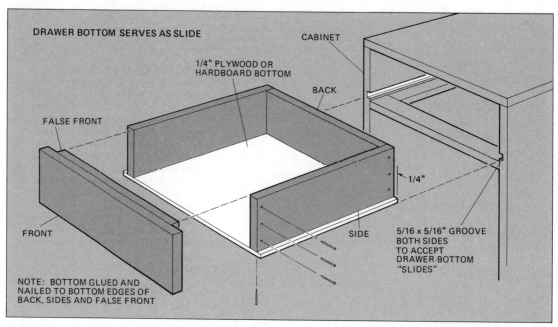

DRAWER BOTTOM SERVES AS SLIDE

1/4" PLYWOOD OR HARDBOARD BOTTOM

CABINET

BACK

FALSE FRONT

FRONT

SIDE

1/4"

5/16 x 5/16" GROOVE BOTH SIDES TO ACCEPT DRAWER-BOTTOM "SLIDES"

NOTE: BOTTOM GLUED AND NAILED TO BOTTOM EDGES OF BACK, SIDES AND FALSE FRONT

A GOOD STUNT—when drawer appearance is not of primary concern—is to build in runners merely by extending the drawer bottom on both sides. This creates slides which ride in corresponding grooves that are cut in the cabinet sides. In this case, it is best to use 1/4-in. hardboard for the drawer bottom. For troublefree sliding, keep the grooves clean and spray them periodically with silicone to prevent sticking.

COMMERCIAL SLIDES are available in bottom and side-mount styles (both shown at right). The bottom-mount type is easiest to install; version shown in drawing is screw-fastened to drawer bottom (at center) as well as to cabinet rail and cabinet back. Less expensive types feature a single roller fastened to the back of the drawer.

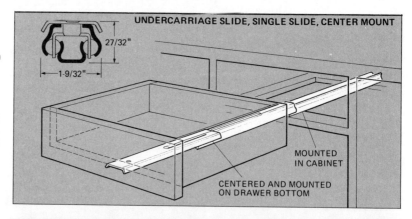

UNDERCARRIAGE SLIDE, SINGLE SLIDE, CENTER MOUNT

27/32"

1-9/32"

MOUNTED IN CABINET

CENTERED AND MOUNTED ON DRAWER BOTTOM

SIDE-MOUNT hardware at right can be used to add a drawer beneath a countertop; units operate the same as side-mounts installed in a cabinet. When using factory-made slides, clearance for hardware must be made when building the drawer (drawer must be narrower). Whether using side or bottom-mount slides, always read the maker's instructions before you begin laying out your drawer.

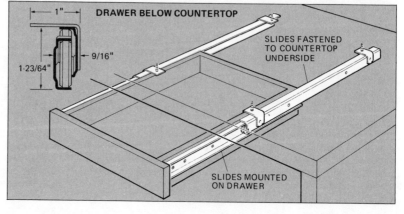

DRAWER BELOW COUNTERTOP

1"

9/16"

1-23/64"

SLIDES FASTENED TO COUNTERTOP UNDERSIDE

SLIDES MOUNTED ON DRAWER

Roll-out shoe drawer

■ THIS ROLL-OUT shoe drawer is designed to accommodate two common metal shoe racks. It rolls smoothly on a metal drawer track and seven nylon rollers. Cut off about 4 in. from the shoe-rack legs, leaving 1¼ in. for attaching with half-round clamps. At the front the racks are clamped directly to the back of the front uprights; at the rear the uprights have to be notched slightly in four places. Cover the sides, top and drawer front with ⅛-in. perforated hardboard to provide ventilation.

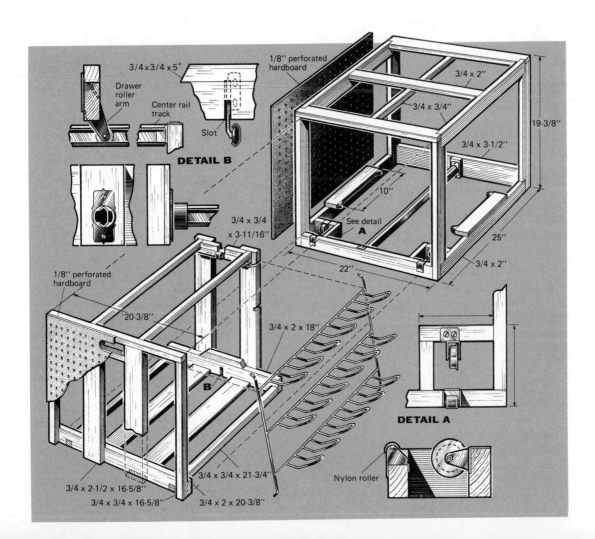

3/4 x 3/4 x 5"
1/8" perforated hardboard
Drawer roller arm
Center rail track
Slot
DETAIL B
3/4 x 2"
3/4 x 3/4"
19-3/8"
3/4 x 3-1/2"
10"
See detail A
3/4 x 3/4 x 3-11/16"
25"
3/4 x 2"
22"
1/8" perforated hardboard
20-3/8"
3/4 x 2 x 18"
B
DETAIL A
3/4 x 2-1/2 x 16-5/8"
3/4 x 3/4 x 16-5/8"
3/4 x 2 x 20-3/8"
3/4 x 3/4 x 21-3/4"
Nylon roller

Lightbox you can build inexpensively

■ CRAFTSMEN, draftsmen or youngsters will find a lightbox to be the handiest thing ever for tracing and drawing. And photographers won't find a better slide viewer for the money.

Actually, it's more than a lightbox; it's also a portable drawing table in that it has a tilting top, built-in measuring rules along three edges and a 24-in. T-square. Two 15-w. fluorescent fixtures, plus two 40-w. showcase lamps, provide even lighting over the entire frosted-glass top.

The unit consists of three separate assemblies: a base, box and cover. The base consists of two bandsawed hardwood side members, which are joined front and back with two 1 x 23½-in. dow-

els shouldered at the ends to glue in ½-in. holes. A 1 x 2¼ x 23½-in. stretcher across the back (part X) is notched at the ends to receive the side members and also provide tilting clearance for the lampbox. The locking bracket for the tilting box is later attached to this stretcher. Holes are made in the base members for a ½ x 23-in. metal shaft which passes through the lampbox to pivot it to the base. The shaft is drilled for two 1-in. No. 6 screws which anchor the shaft to the inside of the lampbox and keep it from shifting sideways. A 1⅛-in. washer cut from ⅛-in. hardboard is placed on the shaft between lampbox and base members.

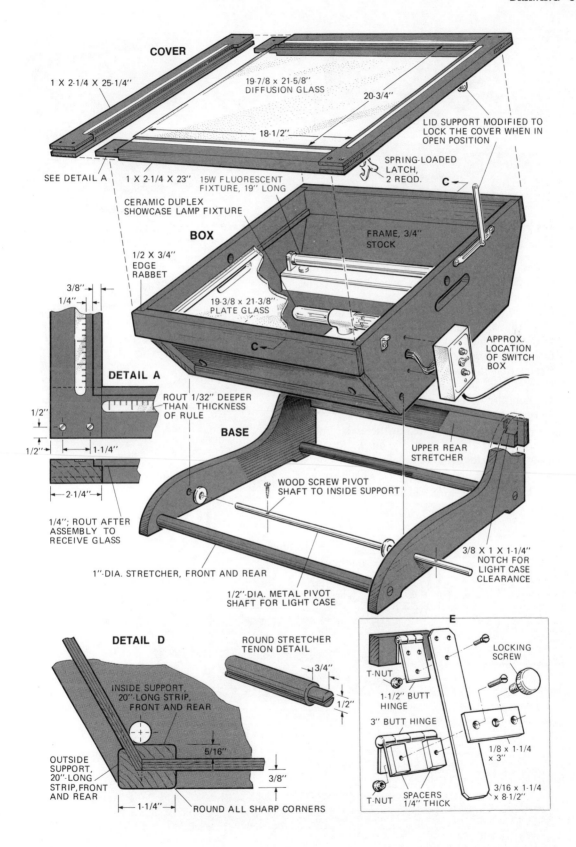

COVER

1 X 2-1/4 X 25-1/4''

19-7/8 x 21-5/8''
DIFFUSION GLASS

20-3/4''

18-1/2''

LID SUPPORT MODIFIED TO
LOCK THE COVER WHEN IN
OPEN POSITION

SEE DETAIL A

1 X 2-1/4 X 23''

15W FLUORESCENT
FIXTURE, 19'' LONG

CERAMIC DUPLEX
SHOWCASE LAMP FIXTURE

SPRING-LOADED
LATCH,
2 REQD.

C ←

BOX

FRAME, 3/4''
STOCK

1/2 X 3/4''
EDGE
RABBET

3/8''

1/4''

19-3/8 x 21-3/8''
PLATE GLASS

C ←

APPROX.
LOCATION
OF SWITCH
BOX

DETAIL A

ROUT 1/32'' DEEPER
THAN THICKNESS
OF RULE

1/2''

BASE

1/2''

1-1/4''

UPPER REAR
STRETCHER

2-1/4''

1/4''; ROUT AFTER
ASSEMBLY TO
RECEIVE GLASS

WOOD SCREW PIVOT
SHAFT TO INSIDE SUPPORT

1''-DIA. STRETCHER, FRONT AND REAR

1/2''-DIA. METAL PIVOT
SHAFT FOR LIGHT CASE

3/8 X 1 X 1-1/4''
NOTCH FOR
LIGHT CASE
CLEARANCE

DETAIL D

ROUND STRETCHER
TENON DETAIL

3/4''

INSIDE SUPPORT,
20''-LONG STRIP,
FRONT AND REAR

1/2''

E

LOCKING
SCREW

T-NUT

5/16''

1-1/2'' BUTT
HINGE

OUTSIDE
SUPPORT,
20''-LONG
STRIP, FRONT
AND REAR

3/8''

3'' BUTT HINGE

1/8 x 1-1/4
x 3''

1-1/4''

ROUND ALL SHARP CORNERS

T-NUT

SPACERS
1/4'' THICK

3/16 x 1-1/4
x 8-1/2''

THE BIG VIEWING SURFACE holds over 100 slides at a time. Fluorescent lamps provide illumination.

THE LAMPBOX INTERIOR is painted white, first with undercoater, then with two coats of enamel.

The two sides of the lampbox are cut from ¾-in. plywood. A ¼ x ¼-in. groove is routed in the inside faces ⅜-in. in from the edges to house the ¼-in. plywood panels which form the bottom, front and back members. The lower edges of the front and back panels are beveled 30° to butt against square edges of the bottom panel. Notice that the two sides of the box have air holes in them and hand holes. Study detail D to see how the beveled joint is sandwiched front and back, between two cleats. Two 1 x 2¼ x 21½-in. stretchers, notched at the ends, brace the box at the top, front and back. Shallow grooves cut in the lower edges of these stretchers let in the front and back panels. There are air holes in these pieces, two in front and two in the

THE COVER is fitted with a desk-lid support, which has been modified to lock in an open position.

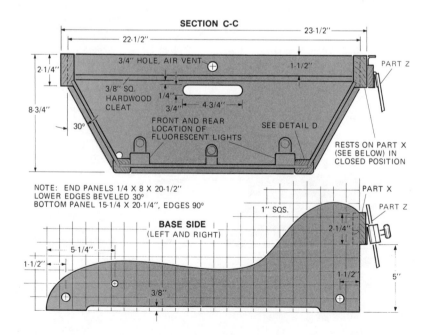

SECTION C-C

22-1/2''   23-1/2''

2-1/4''   3/4'' HOLE, AIR VENT   1-1/2''   PART Z

8-3/4''   3/8'' SQ. HARDWOOD CLEAT   1/4''   4-3/4''   3/4''

30°   FRONT AND REAR LOCATION OF FLUORESCENT LIGHTS   SEE DETAIL D   RESTS ON PART X (SEE BELOW) IN CLOSED POSITION

NOTE: END PANELS 1/4 X 8 X 20-1/2'' LOWER EDGES BEVELED 30° BOTTOM PANEL 15-1/4 X 20-1/4'', EDGES 90°

PART X

1'' SQS.   PART Z

BASE SIDE
(LEFT AND RIGHT)   2-1/4''

5-1/4''

1-1/2''   1-1/2''   5''

3/8''

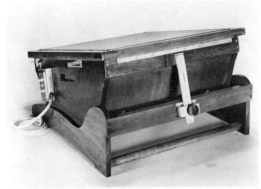

A BRACKET lets you tilt the glass top when the box is used as a tracing table. A knob locks it securely.

A PLYWOOD TEMPLATE, tacked to the faces of the lampbox sides, guides router in running ¼-in. grooves.

A PLUG CUTTER forms the tenons on the ends of the dowel stretchers. A bench saw cuts the shoulders.

A DADO HEAD is used to run ¼-in. grooves in the front and back rails. The arbor is tilted 30°.

back. The plate-glass top rests on ⅜ x ⅜-in. cleats nailed and glued to the ends 1½ in. down.

Section C-C shows the position of the two fluorescent fixtures, and the two showcase lamps which are centered between them. The lamps are wired to toggle and pushbutton switches mounted in a box attached to the right side of the lampbox. The switch box is a wire-mold type, 1 in. thick. Center-drill the cover with a ½-in. drill and cut the additional holes with hole cutters.

Pushbuttons control the fluorescents, the toggle the showcase lamps. Both fluorescents are used for normal density, only one for extreme transparency. All of the lamps are used when the slide or negative is extremely dense.

The cover is a four-sided frame joined at the corners with an open mortise and tenon and rabbeted like a picture frame to receive flush a 19⅜ x 21⅜-in. piece of ¼-in. plate glass. A turnbutton at each corner holds the glass in place. The cover is hinged to the lampbox with a

long piano hinge, and a lid support, modified to suit, locks the cover open when necessary. If you use the same type of lid support used here, you can file a notch in the lower edge of the slotted track and the lid will lock automatically.

A spring-loaded elbow catch holds the cover shut, and a strip of cloth adhesive tape stuck to the front edge of the diffusion glass provides a tab for removing the glass. The self-sticking tape-line rules, which are added to three sides of the cover, are recessed and cemented in routed grooves as shown in detail A.

The hinged bracket for holding the lightbox at the desired angle is shown in detail E. Pivoted by two hinges, it consists of a sliding flat strip (part Z) held by a locking thumbscrew. The 1½-in. butt is attached to a block glued to the lampbox while the 3-in. butt is attached to the base stretcher. A tapped hole through a crossplate receives the thumbscrew.

Draw better plans

Device for drawing perspectives

When you're planning a shop project, a perspective drawing will give you a good idea of the completed project's three-dimensional appearance. This simple guide helps maintain the correct perspective in a drawing, whether you're designing furniture or sketching a landscape.

The only materials you'll need are: two yardsticks or similarly sized pieces of wood, ¾ x 2½ x 54-in. main support of pine, two ¾-in. No. 8 wood screws to secure the yardsticks to the support, two small scraps of sheet steel or sheet aluminum and six thumbtacks. The last two materials fasten the device to the drawing board.

To use this device, secure it and drawing paper to the board. Use a T-square to draw horizontal lines, and a right-angle triangle to draw vertical lines. Use the yardsticks as guides in drawing lines that go back to the predetermined vanishing points—the far ends of the yardsticks.

To store the device, slip a rubber band around the yardsticks to hold them to the main support. Store it in a closet, or hang it on a nail from a hole bored in one end of the support.

Permanent grid for enlarging

Project plans involving curves and unusual shapes are often placed on grids. When enlarging such a plan, you must first draw a full-size grid. Then you draw in the plan, using the placement of the lines on the original as a guide to line placement within the squares of the full-size grid.

You can save time by accurately drawing a permanent full-size grid on poster board. Then lay a sheet of tracing paper over the grid to enlarge a plan. Your work will be uncluttered by squares, and you can use the grid indefinitely. Two grids, one of ½-in. squares and one of 1-in. squares, will serve most needs.

You can also draw an original grid on 8½ x 14-in. paper and make extras on a duplicating machine if you prefer to draw directly on the grid. You should note, however, that the grid copied on a duplicating machine may be somewhat larger than the original. It may be necessary for you to change the sizes of other project parts slightly.

A PERSPECTIVE DEVICE, T-square, right-angle triangle and a sharp pencil can help you make accurate perspective drawings.

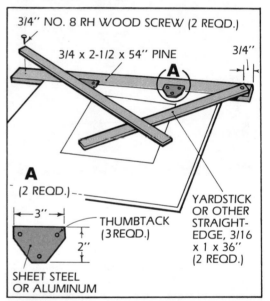

3/4" NO. 8 RH WOOD SCREW (2 REQD.)

3/4 x 2-1/2 x 54" PINE

3/4"

A

A (2 REQD.)

3"

2"

THUMBTACK (3 REQD.)

SHEET STEEL OR ALUMINUM

YARDSTICK OR OTHER STRAIGHT-EDGE, 3/16 x 1 x 36" (2 REQD.)

A PERMANENT GRID will eliminate the need to redraw a grid each time you enlarge a plan. Draw the new plan on tracing paper that's placed over the permanent grid.

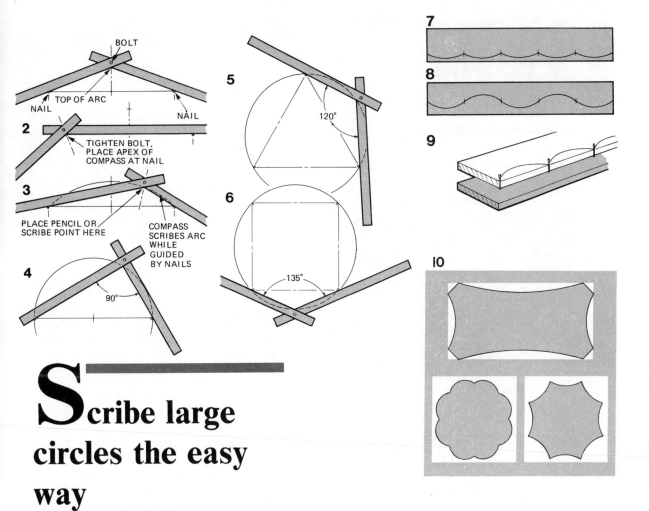

Scribe large circles the easy way

■ THE EASY-TO-MAKE compass lets you draw arcs that would be impossible with a conventional compass. It is constructed of two strips of wood hinged as shown with a nut and bolt. Each leg should be slightly longer than the distance from one end of the planned arc to the other.

1. To use the compass, put brads or nails where you want the arc's end points. Draw a straight line to connect them and mark the high point of the arc. Place bottom of the compass legs against the nails and adjust the compass until its apex is at the arc's high point. Tighten the bolt.

2. Place the apex at one of the nails

3. Hold a pencil at the apex and move compass legs across the nails, maintaining contact at all times.

4. Compass legs can also be set at specific angles. Set at 90°, the compass will scribe perfect circles or semicircles.

5. By setting the compass at 120° and positioning the nails to make an equilateral triangle, it will scribe a complete circle if used on each pairing of nails successively.

6. Similarly, the compass set at 135° scribes a circle if four nails are positioned to form a square. The last two examples are useful when laying out a circle for a walk or driveway if an obstruction prevents the use of a center point. Using four nails (or stakes for large outdoor projects), as opposed to two or three, makes compass use easier since the compass legs can be made shorter.

7, 8. Other uses include the making of scalloped patterns and wavy lines. Be sure to place nails at equal intervals and in a straight line.

9. If the guide nails for a desired pattern need to be positioned on the workpiece edge, use a second board to hold the nails.

10. Decorative shapes can also be laid out.

Fun with a doodling engraver

A FINE ballpoint pen is used to form a design on cardboard taped to a wood wheel. For scribing metal, use a diamond stylus

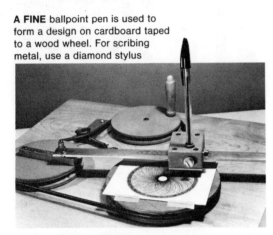

■ IF YOU LIKE TO DOODLE, you'll love the way you can do it with this updated version of an old-time polygraph machine. It uses a ballpoint pen for paper or a diamond-point, abrasive-wheel dresser for metal. All you do is turn a crank and watch the design appear like magic.

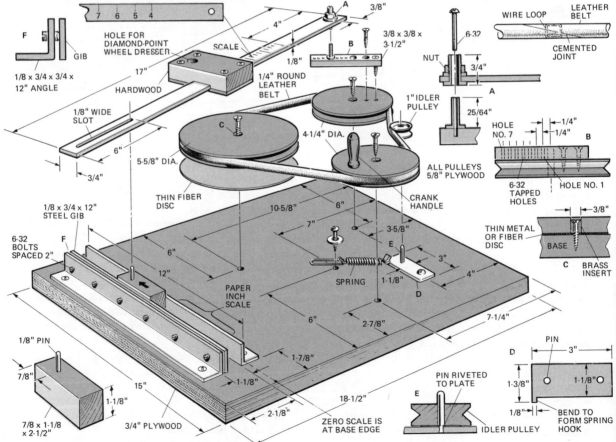

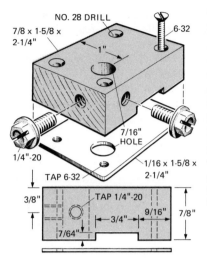

THIS HANDSOME clock dial, an example of the use of metal designs, was engraved in wire-brushed aluminum

THE CIRCULAR design on this trinket-box lid was given a ground finish with abrasive grains and then inset in the lid

Basically, the machine consists of three plywood wheels connected by a leather belt. Bits of masking tape attach the item to be decorated to the wheel, which acts as a rotating "drawing board." As this wheel turns, a block carrying the stylus (diamond tool or pen) moves over it, guided by the stylus arm.

The rotating wheel draws circles; the stylus arm draws oval figures. The combination of these two kinds of curves forms a decorative, usually symmetrical, pattern. Patterns are easily varied by changing the position of the pin that guides the stylus arm, the position of the stylus block along the arm, or the distance of the pivot point from the center of the wheel that operates the stylus arm.

The relative sizes of pivot wheel and pattern-holding wheel, as well as distance of stylus from centerline of arm and effective arm length, also determine the pattern.

The machine's base is a piece of ¾-in. plywood. (Locations of the various parts are given in relation to bottom and right-hand edges when the crank wheel faces the operator.)

You can turn the wheels from ⅝-in. fir plywood and groove the edges for ¼-in. round

THE INDEX mark on the guide block is set by the inch scale

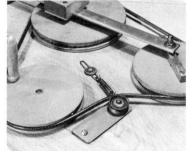

A SPRING-LOADED idler pulley keeps the belt taut and slip free

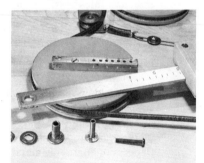

THESE are parts of the pivot assembly linking the stylus and the wood wheel

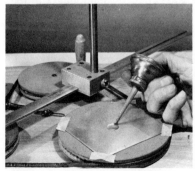

LIGHT oil applied to the metal surface beforehand reduces stylus friction

TABS OF masking tape at the corners hold the metal plate flat

ADDED WEIGHT on the stylus arm lets the diamond cut the brass deeper

leather belts. Each wheel bearing consists of a brass insert drilled to rotate snugly around a No. 6 wood screw. You can improve the wheel action by placing a thin washer of cardboard-like fiber between the wheel and the base.

Use a round leather sewing-machine belt, splice the ends as shown and use household cement and a wire-loop reinforcement to hold them in place. A coating of stick-type belt dressing will help to reduce the slipping.

A 1-in. idler pulley turns on a pin riveted to a thin steel plate, and a coil tension spring holds the pulley against the belt. An elongated wire loop clamped by a wood screw and washer anchors the spring.

The stylus has a ⅛ x 6-in. slot extending almost to one end. A ⅜-in. hole at the opposite end accepts the pivot assembly, which operates the stylus arm.

The steel crank bar has a series of 6-32 tapped holes on ¼-in. centers and is mounted so that hole No. 1 is ¼ in. from the wheel center. For small designs, an additional hole nearer the center is useful.

Maple block holds stylus

A maple block grooved on the bottom holds the stylus. Depth of the groove is slightly less than arm thickness, so when the four 6-32 bolts are tightened, the block is locked securely on the arm.

Bore a $7/16$-in. hole almost tangent to the groove to accept a diamond-tipped, abrasive-wheel dresser. The block can hold other tools, such as a ballpoint pen if built up with a piece of rubber tubing.

The weight of the stylus arm and block is sufficient for holding a ballpoint pen in contact with paper. For engraving metal, additional weight is required. Milling cutters (which weigh about 1½ lbs.) slipped over the diamond-tipped rod will do the trick although any similar weight may be used.

The maple arm-guide block rests in a channel formed by two pieces of metal angle. A gib positioned between the block and left-hand angle is used to lock the block in a fixed position. One bolt enters a hole drilled about halfway through the gib to prevent endwise slippage.

The block's pin engages the slot in the stylus arm and is positioned somewhat nearer one end of the block than the other. Reverse the block and a greater range of pin position can be obtained in one direction. At the block's midpoint, on each side, is an index mark for positioning the block relative to a scale. An arrow on top of the block points normally to the rear edge of the base.

Three scales enable setting for repeat drawing of a particular design.

■ An inch scale 13-in. long is glued to the outer vertical surface of the right-hand metal angle 3 in. from the end for gauging the position of sliding block.

■ An inch scale, with ¼-in. divisions, is stamped along the top of the stylus arm, with the "0" position coinciding with the center of the pivot hole over the pulley. Only the portion from 4 to 8 in. is needed. The right-hand edge of the block is used as an index line in setting the position of the stylus.

■ A series of numbers—1, 3, 5 and 7—identify the tapped holes along the top of the steel bar. These numbers, with No. 1 hole near pulley center, indicate different positions of the stylus-arm pivot with respect to the axis of the pulley.

Record design's 'formula'

Once a design has been worked out by trial, record its "formula" by writing down the three scale readings in left-to-right sequence. For example, 7, 5¾, 6 indicates that the guide block is at 7 in., the stylus-holding block is at 5¾ in. and the arm pivot is at hole No. 6. If desired, an arrow pointing upward for the "normal" position of the block, or downward for the reversed position, can be added to the formula.

Aluminum is easy to engrave; brass requires more pressure. Best pressure for various metals can be found by trial. Actually, when using a rounded diamond or other point, the "engraving" is more of a rubbing than a cutting action.

The metal blank should be flat. Its surface can be prepared in various ways, ranging from polishing to dulling by chemical etching or rubbing with a mixture of abrasive grit and water. For a ground-glass effect on aluminum, rub 180-grit aluminum-oxide grains mixed with water over the surface with a small metal block.

Fasten the blank with self-adhering tape and spread a thin layer of oil over the surface to reduce stylus friction. Bring the stylus against the blank with the arm elevated slightly above the guide block. Put additional weights in place, then turn the guide pulley slowly. Count the number of revolutions the wheel requires to create a pattern and record it along with the "formula." Best starting and stopping points for the stylus tip are on the smallest diameter of a pattern.

INDEX · VOLUME 7

SHOP GUIDE

CUSTOMARY TO METRIC (CONVERSION) Conversion factors can be carried so far they become impractical. In cases below where an entry is exact it is followed by an asterisk (*). Where considerable rounding off has taken place, the entry is followed by a + or a − sign.

Linear Measure

inches	millimeters
1/16	1.5875*
1/8	3.2
3/16	4.8
1/4	6.35*
5/16	7.9
3/8	9.5
7/16	11.1
1/2	12.7*
9/16	14.3
5/8	15.9
11/16	17.5
3/4	19.05*
13/16	20.6
7/8	22.2
15/16	23.8
1	25.4*

inches	centimeters
1	2.54*
2	5.1
3	7.6
4	10.2
5	12.7*
6	15.2
7	17.8
8	20.3
9	22.9
10	25.4*
11	27.9
12	30.5

feet	centimeters	meters
1	30.48*	.3048*
2	61	.61
3	91	.91
4	122	1.22
5	152	1.52
6	183	1.83
7	213	2.13
8	244	2.44
9	274	2.74
10	305	3.05
50	1524*	15.24*
100	3048*	30.48*

1 yard = .9144* meters
1 rod = 5.0292* meters
1 mile = 1.6 kilometers
1 nautical mile = 1.852* kilometers

Weights

ounces	grams
1	28.3
2	56.7
3	85
4	113
5	142
6	170
7	198
8	227
9	255
10	283
11	312
12	340
13	369
14	397
15	425
16	454

Formula (exact):
ounces × 28.349 523 125* = grams

pounds	kilograms
1	.45
2	.9
3	1.4
4	1.8
5	2.3
6	2.7
7	3.2
8	3.6
9	4.1
10	4.5

1 short ton (2000 lbs) = 907 kilograms (kg)
Formula (exact):
pounds × .453 592 37* = kilograms

Fluid Measure

(Milliliters [ml] and cubic centimeters [cc] are equivalent, but it is customary to use milliliters for liquids.)

1 cu in	= 16.39 ml
1 fl oz	= 29.6 ml
1 cup	= 237 ml
1 pint	= 473 ml
1 quart	= 946 ml
	= .946 liters
1 gallon	= 3785 ml
	= 3.785 liters

Formula (exact):
fluid ounces × 29.573 529 562 5* = milliliters

Volume

1 cu in	= 16.39 cubic centimeters (cc)
1 cu ft	= 28 316.7 cc
1 bushel	= 35 239.1 cc
1 peck	= 8 809.8 cc

Area

1 sq in	= 6.45 sq cm
1 sq ft	= 929 sq cm
	= .093 sq meters
1 sq yd	= .84 sq meters
1 acre	= 4 046.9 sq meters
	= .404 7 hectares
1 sq mile	= 2 589 988 sq meters
	= 259 hectares
	= 2.589 9 sq kilometers

Miscellaneous

1 British thermal unit (Btu) (mean) = 1 055.9 joules
1 horsepower = 745.7 watts = .75 kilowatts
caliber (diameter of a firearm's bore in hundredths of an inch) = .254 millimeters (mm)

1 atmosphere pressure = 101 325* pascals (newtons per sq meter)
1 pound per square inch (psi) = 6 895 pascals
1 pound per square foot = 47.9 pascals
1 knot = 1.85 kilometers per hour
1 mile per hour = 1.6093 kilometers per hour